JOAN OF NAPLES

1343-1382

by

Alexandre Dumas

Copyright © 2012 Read Books Ltd.
This book is copyright and may not be
reproduced or copied in any way without
the express permission of the publisher in writing

British Library Cataloguing-in-Publication Data
A catalogue record for this book is available from the
British Library

Contents

Alexandre Dumas 5

CHAPTER I 7

CHAPTER II. 26

CHAPTER III 47

CHAPTER IV 70

CHAPTER V 88

CHAPTER VI 108

CHAPTER VII 123

CHAPTER VIII 139

Alexandre Dumas

Alexandre Dumas was born in Villers-Cotterêts, France in 1802. His parents were poor, but their heritage and good reputation – Alexandre's father had been a general in Napoleon's army – provided Alexandre with opportunities for good employment. In 1822, Dumas moved to Paris to work for future king Louis Philippe I in the Palais Royal. It was here that he began to write for magazines and the theatre.

In 1829 and 1830 respectively, Dumas produced the plays Henry III and His Court and Christine, both of which met with critical acclaim and financial success. As a result, he was able to commit himself full-time to writing. Despite the turbulent economic times which followed the Revolution of 1830, Dumas turned out to have something of an entrepreneurial streak, and did well for himself in this decade. He founded a production studio that turned out hundreds of stories under his creative direction, and began to produce serialised novels for newspapers which were widely read by the French public. It was over the next two decades, as a now famous and much loved author of romantic and adventuring sagas, that Dumas produced his best-known works – the D'Artagnan romances, including The Three Musketeers, in 1844, and The Count of Monte Cristo, in 1846.

Dumas made a lot of money from his writing, but he was almost constantly penniless as a result of his extravagant lifestyle and love of women. In 1851 he fled his creditors to Belgium, and then Russia, and then Italy, not returning to Paris until 1864. Dumas died in Puys, France, in 1870, at the age of 68. He is now enshrined in the Panthéon of Paris alongside fellow authors Victor Hugo and Emile Zola. Since his death, his fiction has been translated into almost a hundred languages, and has formed the basis for more than 200 motion pictures.

CHAPTER I

In the night of the 15th of January 1343, while the inhabitants of Naples lay wrapped in peaceful slumber, they were suddenly awakened by the bells of the three hundred churches that this thrice blessed capital contains. In the midst of the disturbance caused by so rude a call the first thought in the mind of all was that the town was on fire, or that the army of some enemy had mysteriously landed under cover of night and could put the citizens to the edge of the sword. But the doleful, intermittent sounds of all these fills, which disturbed the silence at regular and distant intervals, were an invitation to the faithful to pray for a passing soul, and it was soon evident that no disaster threatened the town, but that the king alone was in danger.

Indeed, it had been plain for several days past that the greatest uneasiness prevailed in Castel Nuovo; the officers of the crown were assembled regularly twice a day, and persons of importance, whose right it was to make their way into the king's apartments, came out evidently bowed down with grief. But although the king's death was regarded as a misfortune that nothing could avert, yet the whole town, on learning for certain of the approach of his last hour, was affected with a sincere grief, easily understood when one learns that the man about to die, after a reign of thirty-three years, eight months, and a few days, was Robert of Anjou, the most wise, just, and glorious king who had ever sat on the throne of Sicily. And so he carried with him to the tomb the eulogies and regrets of all his subjects.

Soldiers would speak with enthusiasm of the long wars he had waged with Frederic and Peter of Aragon, against Henry VII and Louis of Bavaria; and felt their hearts beat high, remembering the glories of campaigns in Lombardy and Tuscany; priests would gratefully extol his constant defence of the papacy against Ghibelline attacks, and the founding of convents, hospitals, and churches throughout his kingdom; in the world of letters he was regarded as the most learned king in Christendom; Petrarch, indeed, would receive the poet's crown from no other hand, and had spent three consecutive days answering all the questions that Robert had deigned to ask him on every topic of human knowledge. The men of law, astonished by the wisdom of those laws which now enriched the Neapolitan code, had dubbed him the Solomon of their day; the nobles applauded him for protecting their ancient privileges, and the people were eloquent of his clemency, piety, and mildness. In a word, priests and soldiers, philosophers and poets, nobles and peasants, trembled when they thought that the government was to fall into the hands of a foreigner and of a young girl, recalling those words of Robert, who, as he followed in the funeral train of Charles, his only son, turned as he reached the threshold of the church and sobbingly exclaimed to his barons about him, "This day the crown has fallen from my head: alas for me! alas for you!"

Now that the bells were ringing for the dying moments of the good king, every mind was full of these prophetic words: women prayed fervently to God; men from all parts of the town bent their steps towards the royal palace to get the earliest and most authentic news, and after waiting some moments, passed in exchanging sad reflections, were obliged to return as they had come, since nothing that went on in the privacy of the family found its way outside—the castle was plunged in complete darkness, the drawbridge was raised as usual, and the guards were at their post.

Yet if our readers care to be present at the death of the nephew of Saint Louis and the grandson of Charles of Anjou, we may conduct them into the chamber of the dying man. An alabaster lamp suspended from the ceiling serves to light the vast and sombre room, with walls draped in black velvet sewn with golden fleur-de-lys. Near the wall which faces the two entrance doors that at this moment are both shut close, there stands beneath a brocaded canopy an ebony bed, supported on four twisted columns carved with symbolic figures. The king, after a struggle with a violent paroxysm, has fallen swooning in the arms of his confessor and his doctor, who each hold one of his dying hands, feeling his pulse anxiously and exchanging looks of intelligence. At the foot of the bed stands a woman about fifty years of age, her hands clasped, her eyes raised to heaven, in an attitude of resigned grief: this woman is the queen, No tears dim her eyes: her sunken cheek has that waxen yellow tinge that one sees on the bodies of saints preserved by miracle. In her look is that mingling of calm and suffering that points to a soul at once tried by sorrow and imbued with religion. After the lapse of an hour, while no movement had disturbed the profound silence which reigned about the bed of death, the king trembled slightly; opened his eyes, and endeavoured feebly to raise his head. They thanking the physician and priest with a smile, who had both hastened to arrange his pillows, he begged the queen to come near, and told her in a low voice that he would speak with her a moment alone. The doctor and confessor retired, deeply bowing, and the king followed them with his eyes up to the moment when one of the doors closed behind them. He passed his hand across his brow, as though seeking to collect his thoughts, and rallying all his forces for the supreme effort, pronounced these words:

"What I must say to you, Sancha, has no concern with those two good persons who were here a moment ago: their task is ended. One has done all for my body that human science could teach him, and all that has come of it is that my death is yet a little deferred; the other has now absolved me of all my sins, and assured me of God's forgiveness, yet cannot keep from me those dread apparitions which in this terrible hour arise before me. Twice have you seen me battling with a superhuman horror. My brow has been bathed in sweat, my limbs rigid, my cries have been stifled by a hand of iron. Has God permitted the Evil Spirit to tempt me? Is this remorse in phantom shape? These two conflicts I have suffered have so subdued my strength that I can never endure a third. Listen then, my Sandra, for I have instructions to give you on which perhaps the safety of my soul depends."

"My lord and my master," said the queen in the most gentle accents of submission, "I am ready to listen to your orders; and should it be that God, in the hidden designs of His providence, has willed to call you to His glory while we are plunged in grief, your last wishes shall be fulfilled here on earth most scrupulously and exactly. But," she added, with all the solicitude of a timid soul, "pray suffer me to sprinkle drops of holy water and banish the accursed one from this chamber, and let me offer up some part of that service of prayer that you composed in honour of your sainted brother to implore God's protection in this hour when we can ill afford to lose it."

Then opening a richly bound book, she read with fervent devotion certain verses of the office that Robert had written in a very pure Latin for his brother Louis, Bishop of Toulouse, which was in use in the Church as late as the time of the Council of Trent.

Soothed by the charm of the prayers he had himself composed, the king was near forgetting the object of the interview he had so solemnly and eagerly demanded and letting himself lapse into a state of vague melancholy, he murmured in a subdued voice, "Yes, yes, you are right; pray for me, for you too are a saint, and I am but a poor sinful man."

"Say not so, my lord," interrupted Dona Sancha; "you are the greatest, wisest, and most just king who has ever sat upon the throne of Naples."

"But the throne is usurped," replied Robert in a voice of gloom; "you know that the kingdom belonged to my elder brother, Charles Martel; and since Charles was on the throne of Hungary, which he inherited from his mother, the kingdom of Naples devolved by right upon his eldest son, Carobert, and not on me, who am the third in rank of the family. And I have suffered myself to be crowned in my nephew's stead, though he was the only lawful-king; I have put the younger branch in the place of the elder, and for thirty-three years I have stifled the reproaches of my conscience. True, I have won battles, made laws, founded churches; but a single word serves to give the lie to all the pompous titles showered upon me by the people's admiration, and this one word rings out clearer in my ears than all the flattery of courtiers, all the songs of poets, all the orations of the crowd:—I am an usurper!"

"Be not unjust towards yourself, my lord, and bear in mind that if you did not abdicate in favour of the rightful heir, it was because you wished to save the people from the worst misfortunes. Moreover," continued the queen, with that air of profound conviction that an unanswerable argument inspires, "you have remained king by the consent and authority of our Holy Father the sovereign pontiff, who disposes of the throne as a fief belonging to the Church."

"I have long quieted my scruples thus," replied the dying man, "and the pope's authority has kept me silent; but whatever security one may pretend to feel in one's lifetime, there yet comes a dreadful solemn hour when all illusions needs must vanish: this hour for me has come, and now I must appear before God, the one unfailing judge."

"If His justice cannot fail, is not His mercy infinite?"

pursued the queen, with the glow of sacred inspiration. "Even if there were good reason for the fear that has shaken your soul, what fault could not be effaced by a repentance so noble? Have you not repaired the wrong you may have done your nephew Carobert, by bringing his younger son Andre to your kingdom and marrying him to Joan, your poor Charles's elder daughter? Will not they inherit your crown?"

"Alas!" cried Robert, with a deep sigh, "God is punishing me perhaps for thinking too late of this just reparation. O my good and noble Sandra, you touch a chord which vibrates sadly in my heart, and you anticipate the unhappy confidence I was about to make. I feel a gloomy presentiment—and in the hour of death presentiment is prophecy—that the two sons of my nephew, Louis, who has been King of Hungary since his father died, and Andre, whom I desired to make King of Naples, will prove the scourge of my family. Ever since Andre set foot in our castle, a strange fatality has pursued and overturned my projects. I had hoped that if Andre and Joan were brought up together a tender intimacy would arise between the two children; and that the beauty of our skies, our civilisation, and the attractions of our court would end by softening whatever rudeness there might be in the young Hungarian's character; but in spite of my efforts all has tended to cause coldness, and even aversion, between the bridal pair. Joan, scarcely fifteen, is far ahead of her age. Gifted with a brilliant and mobile mind, a noble and lofty character, a lively and glowing fancy, now free and frolicsome as a child, now grave and proud as a queen, trustful and simple as a young girl, passionate and sensitive as a woman, she presents the most striking contrast to Andre, who, after a stay of ten years at our court, is wilder, more gloomy, more intractable than ever. His cold, regular features, impassive countenance, and indifference to every pleasure that his wife appears to love, all this has raised between him and Joan a barrier of indifference, even of antipathy. To the tenderest effusion his reply is no more than a scornful smile or a frown, and he never seems happier than when on a pretext of the chase he can escape from the court. These, then, are the two, man and wife, on whose heads my crown shall rest, who in a short space will find themselves exposed to every passion whose dull growl is now heard below a deceptive calm, but which only awaits the moment when I breathe my last, to burst forth upon them."

"O my God, my God!" the queen kept repeating in her grief: her arms fell by her side, like the arms of a statue weeping by a tomb.

"Listen, Dona Sandra. I know that your heart has never clung to earthly vanities, and that you only wait till God has called me to Himself to withdraw to the convent of Santa Maria delta Croce, founded by yourself in the hope that you might there end your days. Far be it from me to dissuade you from your sacred vocation, when I am myself descending into the tomb and am conscious of the nothingness of all human greatness. Only grant me one year of widowhood before you pass on to your bridal with the Lord, one year in which you will watch over Joan and her husband, to keep from them all the dangers that threaten. Already the woman who was the seneschal's wife and her son have too much influence over our grand-daughter; be specially careful, and amid the many interests, intrigues, and temptations that will surround the young queen, distrust particularly the affection of Bertrand d'Artois, the beauty of Louis of Tarentum; and the ambition of Charles of Durazzo."

The king paused, exhausted by the effort of speaking; then turning on his wife a supplicating glance and extending his thin wasted hand, he added in a scarcely audible voice:

"Once again I entreat you, leave not the court before a year has passed. Do you promise me?"

"I promise, my lord."

"And now," said Robert, whose face at these words took on a new animation, "call my confessor and the physician and summon the family, for the hour is at hand, and soon I shall not have the strength to speak my last words."

A few moments later the priest and the doctor re-entered the room, their faces bathed, in tears. The king thanked them warmly for their care of him in his last illness, and begged them help to dress him in the coarse garb of a Franciscan monk, that God, as he said, seeing him die in poverty, humility, and penitence, might the more easily grant him pardon. The confessor and doctor placed upon his naked feet the sandals worn by mendicant friars, robed him in a Franciscan frock, and tied the rope about his waist. Stretched thus upon his bed, his brow surmounted by his scanty locks, with his long white beard, and his hands crossed upon his breast, the King of Naples looked like one of those aged anchorites who spend their lives in mortifying the flesh, and whose souls, absorbed in heavenly contemplation, glide insensibly from out their last ecstasy into eternal bliss. Some time he lay thus with closed eyes, putting up a silent prayer to God; then he bade them light the spacious room as for a great solemnity, and gave a sign to the two persons who stood, one at the head, the other at the foot of the bed. The two folding doors opened, and the whole of the royal family, with the queen at their head and the chief barons following, took their places in silence around the dying king to hear his last wishes.

His eyes turned toward Joan, who stood next him on his right hand, with an indescribable look of tenderness and grief. She was of a beauty so unusual and so marvellous, that her grandfather was fascinated by the dazzling sight, and mistook her for an angel that God had sent to console him on his deathbed. The pure lines of her fine profile, her great black liquid eyes, her noble brow uncovered, her hair shining like the raven's wing, her delicate mouth, the whole effect of this beautiful face on the mind of those who beheld her was that of a deep melancholy and sweetness, impressing itself once and for ever. Tall and slender, but without the excessive thinness of some young girls, her movements had that careless supple grace that recall the waving of a flower stalk in the breeze. But in spite of all these smiling and innocent graces one could yet discern in Robert's heiress a will firm and resolute to brave every obstacle, and the dark rings that circled her fine eyes plainly showed that her heart was already agitated by passions beyond her years.

Beside Joan stood her younger sister, Marie, who was twelve or thirteen years of age, the second daughter of Charles, Duke of Calabria, who had died before her birth, and whose mother, Marie of Valois, had unhappily been lost to her from her cradle. Exceedingly pretty and shy, she seemed distressed by such an assembly of great personages, and quietly drew near to the widow of the grand seneschal, Philippa, surnamed the Catanese, the princesses' governess, whom they honoured as a mother. Behind the princesses and beside this lady stood her son, Robert of Cabane, a handsome young man, proud and upright, who with his left hand played with his slight moustache while he secretly cast on Joan a glance of audacious boldness. The group was completed by Dona Cancha, the young chamberwoman to the princesses, and by the Count of Terlizzi, who exchanged with her many a furtive look and many an open smile. The second group was composed of Andre, Joan's husband, and Friar Robert, tutor to the young prince, who had come with him from Budapesth, and never left him for a minute. Andre was at this time perhaps eighteen years old: at first sight one was struck by the extreme regularity of his features, his handsome, noble face, and abundant fair hair; but among all these Italian faces, with their vivid animation, his countenance lacked expression, his eyes seemed dull, and something hard and icy in his looks revealed his wild character and foreign extraction. His tutor's portrait Petrarch has drawn for us: crimson face, hair and beard red, figure short and crooked;

proud in poverty, rich and miserly; like a second Diogenes, with hideous and deformed limbs barely concealed beneath his friar's frock.

In the third group stood the widow of Philip, Prince of Tarentum, the king's brother, honoured at the court of Naples with the title of Empress of Constantinople, a style inherited by her as the granddaughter of Baldwin II. Anyone accustomed to sound the depths of the human heart would at one glance have perceived that this woman under her ghastly pallor concealed an implacable hatred, a venomous jealousy, and an all-devouring ambition. She had her three sons about her—Robert, Philip, and Louis, the youngest. Had the king chosen out from among his nephews the handsomest, bravest, and most generous, there can be no doubt that Louis of Tarentum would have obtained the crown. At the age of twenty-three he had already excelled the cavaliers of most renown in feats of arms; honest, loyal, and brave, he no sooner conceived a project than he promptly carried it out. His brow shone in that clear light which seems to serve as a halo of success to natures so privileged as his; his fine eyes, of a soft and velvety black, subdued the hearts of men who could not resist their charm, and his caressing smile made conquest sweet. A child of destiny, he had but to use his will; some power unknown, some beneficent fairy had watched over his birth, and undertaken to smooth away all obstacles, gratify all desires.

Near to him, but in the fourth group, his cousin Charles of Duras stood and scowled. His mother, Agnes, the widow of the Duke of Durazzo and Albania, another of the king's brothers, looked upon him affrighted, clutching to her breast her two younger sons, Ludovico, Count of Gravina, and Robert, Prince of Morea. Charles, pale-faced, with short hair and thick beard, was glancing with suspicion first at his dying uncle and then at Joan and the little Marie, then again at his cousins, apparently so excited by tumultuous thoughts that he could not stand still. His feverish uneasiness presented a marked contrast with the calm, dreamy face of Bertrand d'Artois, who, giving precedence to his father Charles, approached the queen at the foot of the bed, and so found himself face to face with Joan. The young man was so absorbed by the beauty of the princess that he seemed to see nothing else in the room.

As soon as Joan and Andre, the Princes of Tarentum and Durazzo, the Counts of Artois, and Queen Sancha had taken their places round the bed of death, forming a semicircle, as we have just described, the vice-chancellor passed through the rows of barons, who according to their rank were following closely after the princes of the blood; and bowing low before the king, unfolded a parchment sealed with the royal seal, and read in a solemn voice, amid a profound silence:

"Robert, by the grace of God King of Sicily and Jerusalem, Count of Provence, Forcalquier, and Piedmont, Vicar of the Holy Roman Church, hereby nominates and declares his sole heiress in the kingdom of Sicily on this side and the other side of the strait, as also in the counties of Provence, Forcalquier, and Piedmont, and in all his other territories,

Joan, Duchess of Calabria, elder daughter of the excellent lord Charles, Duke of Calabria, of illustrious memory.

"Moreover, he nominates and declares the honourable lady Marie, younger daughter of the late Duke of Calabria, his heiress in the county of Alba and in the jurisdiction of the valley of Grati and the territory of Giordano, with all their castles and dependencies; and orders that the lady thus named receive them in fief direct from the aforesaid duchess and her heirs; on this condition, however, that if the duchess give and grant to her illustrious sister or to her assigns the sum of 10,000 ounces of gold by way of compensation, the county and jurisdiction aforesaid—shall remain in the possession of the duchess and her heirs.

"Moreover, he wills and commands, for private and secret reasons, that the aforesaid lady Marie shall contract a marriage with the very illustrious prince, Louis, reigning King of Hungary. And in case any impediment should appear to this marriage by reason of the union said to be already arranged and signed between the King of Hungary and the King of Bohemia and his daughter, our lord the king commands that the illustrious lady Marie shall contract a marriage with the elder son of the mighty lord Don Juan, Duke of Normandy, himself the elder son of the reigning King of France."

At this point Charles of Durazzo gave Marie a singularly meaning look, which escaped the notice of all present, their attention being absorbed by the reading of Robert's will. The young girl herself, from the moment when she first heard her own name, had stood confused and thunderstruck, with scarlet cheeks, not daring to raise her eyes.

The vice-chancellor continued:

"Moreover, he has willed and commanded that the counties of Forcalquier and Provence shall in all perpetuity be united to his kingdom, and shall form one sole and inseparable dominion, whether or not there be several sons or daughters or any other reason of any kind for its partition, seeing that this union is of the utmost importance for the security and common prosperity of the kingdom and counties aforesaid.

"Moreover, he has decided and commanded that in case of the death of the Duchess Joan—which God avert!—without lawful issue of her body, the most illustrious lord Andre, Duke of Calabria, her husband, shall have the principality of Salerno, with the title, fruits, revenues, and all the rights thereof, together with the revenue of 2000 ounces of gold for maintenance.

"Moreover, he has decided and ordered that the Queen above all, and also the venerable father Don Philip of Cabassole, Bishop of Cavaillon, vice-chancellor of the kingdom of Sicily, and the magnificent lords Philip of Sanguineto, seneschal of Provence, Godfrey of Marsan, Count of Squillace, admiral of the kingdom, and Charles of Artois, Count of Aire, shall be governors, regents, and administrators of the aforesaid lord Andre and the aforesaid ladies Joan and Marie, until such time as the duke, the duchess, and the very illustrious lady Marie shall have attained their twenty-fifth year," etc. etc.

When the vice-chancellor had finished reading, the king sat up, and glancing round upon his fair and numerous family, thus spoke:

"My children, you have heard my last wishes. I have bidden you all to my deathbed, that you may see how the glory of the world passes away. Those whom men name the great ones of the earth have more duties to perform, and after death more accounts to render: it is in this that their greatness lies. I have reigned thirty-three years, and God before whom I am about to appear, God to whom my sighs have often arisen during my long and painful life, God alone knows the thoughts that rend my heart in the hour of death. Soon shall I be lying in the tomb, and all that remains of me in this world will live in the memory of those who pray for me. But before I leave you for ever, you, oh, you who are twice my daughters, whom I have loved with a double love, and you my nephews who have had from me all the care and affection of a father, promise me to be ever united in heart and in wish, as indeed you are in my love. I have lived longer than your fathers, I the eldest of all, and thus no doubt God has wished to tighten the bonds of your affection, to accustom you to live in one family and to pay honour to one head. I have loved you all alike, as a father should, without exception or preference. I have disposed of my throne according to the law of nature and the inspiration of my conscience: Here are the heirs of the crown of Naples; you, Joan, and you, Andre, will never forget the love and respect that are due between husband and wife, and mutually sworn by you at the foot of the altar; and you, my nephews all; my barons, my officers, render homage to your lawful sovereigns; Andre of Hungary, Louis of Tarentum, Charles of Durazzo, remember that you are brothers; woe to him who shall imitate the perfidy of Cain! May his blood fall upon his own head, and may he be accursed by Heaven as he is by the mouth of a dying man; and may the blessing of the Father, the Son, and the Holy Spirit descend upon that man whose heart is good, when the Lord of mercy shall call to my soul Himself!"

The king remained motionless, his arms raised, his eyes fixed on heaven, his cheeks extraordinarily bright, while the princes, barons, and officers of the court proffered to Joan and her husband the oath of fidelity and allegiance. When it was the turn of the Princes of Duras to advance, Charles disdainfully stalked past Andre, and bending his knee before the princess, said in a loud voice, as he kissed her hand—

"To you, my queen, I pay my homage."

All looks were turned fearfully towards the dying man, but the good king no longer heard. Seeing him fall back rigid and motionless, Dona Sancha burst into sobs, and cried in a voice choked with tears—

"The king is dead; let us pray for his soul."

At the very same moment all the princes hurried from the room, and every passion hitherto suppressed in the presence of the king now found its vent like a mighty torrent breaking through its banks.

"Long live Joan!" Robert of Cabane, Louis of Tarentum, and Bertrand of Artois were the first to exclaim, while the prince's tutor, furiously breaking through the crowd and apostrophising the various members of the council of regency, cried aloud in varying tones of passion, "Gentlemen, you have forgotten the king's wish already; you must cry, 'Long live Andre!' too;" then, wedding example to precept, and himself making more noise than all the barons together, he cried in a voice of thunder—

"Long live the King of Naples!"

But there was no echo to his cry, and Charles of Durazzo, measuring the Dominican with a terrible look, approached the queen, and taking her by the hand, slid back the curtains of the balcony, from which was seen the square and the town of Naples. So far as the eye could reach there stretched an immense crowd, illuminated by streams of light, and thousands of heads were turned upward towards Castel Nuovo to gather any news that might be announced. Charles respectfully drawing back and indicating his fair cousin with his hand, cried out—

"People of Naples, the King is dead: long live the Queen!"

"Long live Joan, Queen of Naples!" replied the people, with a single mighty cry that resounded through every quarter of the town.

The events that on this night had followed each other with the rapidity of a dream had produced so deep an impression on Joan's mind, that, agitated by a thousand different feelings, she retired to her own rooms, and shutting herself up in her chamber, gave free vent to her grief. So long as the conflict of so many ambitions waged about the tomb, the young queen, refusing every consolation that was offered her, wept bitterly for the death of her grandfather, who had loved her to the point of weakness. The king was buried with all solemnity in the church of Santa Chiara, which he had himself founded and dedicated to the Holy Sacrament, enriching it with magnificent frescoes by Giotto and other precious relics, among which is shown still, behind the tribune of the high altar, two columns of white marble taken from Solomon's temple. There still lies Robert, represented on his tomb in the dress of a king and in a monk's frock, on the right of the monument to his son Charles, the Duke of Calabria.

CHAPTER II

As soon as the obsequies were over, Andre's tutor hastily assembled the chief Hungarian lords, and it was decided in a council held in the presence of the prince and with his consent, to send letters to his mother, Elizabeth of Poland, and his brother, Louis of Hungary, to make known to them the purport of Robert's will, and at the same time to lodge a complaint at the court of Avignon against the conduct of the princes and people of Naples in that they had proclaimed Joan alone Queen of Naples, thus overlooking the rights of her husband, and further to demand for him the pope's order for Andre's coronation. Friar Robert, who had not only a profound knowledge of the court intrigues, but also the experience of a philosopher and all a monk's cunning, told his pupil that he ought to profit by the depression of spirit the king's death had produced in Joan, and ought not to suffer her favourites to use this time in influencing her by their seductive counsels.

But Joan's ability to receive consolation was quite as ready as her grief had at first been impetuous; the sobs which seemed to be breaking her heart ceased all at once; new thoughts, more gentle, less lugubrious, took possession of the young queen's mind; the trace of tears vanished, and a smile lit up her liquid eyes like the sun's ray following on rain. This change, anxiously awaited, was soon observed by Joan's chamberwoman: she stole to the queen's room, and falling on her knees, in accents of flattery and affection, she offered her first congratulations to her lovely mistress. Joan opened her arms and held her in a long embrace, for Dona Cancha was far more to her than a lady-in-waiting; she was the companion of infancy, the depositary of all her secrets, the confidante of her most private thoughts. One had but to glance at this young girl to understand the fascination she could scarcely fail to exercise over the queen's mind. She had a frank and smiling countenance, such as inspires confidence and captivates the mind at first sight. Her face had an irresistible charm, with clear blue eyes, warm golden hair, mouth bewitchingly turned up at the corners, and delicate little chin. Wild, happy, light of heart, pleasure and love were the breath of her being; her dainty refinement, her charming inconstancies, all made her at sixteen as lovely as an angel, though at heart she was corrupt. The whole court was at her feet, and Joan felt more affection for her than for her own sister.

"Well, my dear Cancha," she murmured, with a sigh, "you find me very sad and very unhappy!"

"And you find me, fair queen," replied the confidante, fixing an admiring look on Joan,—"you find me just the opposite, very happy that I can lay at your feet before anyone else the proof of the joy that the people of Naples are at this moment feeling. Others perhaps may envy you the crown that shines upon your brow, the throne which is one of the noblest in the world, the shouts of this entire town that sound rather like worship than homage; but I, madam, I envy you your lovely black hair, your dazzling eyes, your more than mortal grace, which make every man adore you."

"And yet you know, my Cancha, I am much to be pitied both as a queen and as a woman: when one is fifteen a crown is heavy to wear, and I have not the liberty of the meanest of my subjects—I mean in my affections; for before I reached an age when I could think I was sacrificed to a man whom I can never love."

"Yet, madam," replied Cancha in a more insinuating voice, "in this court there is a young cavalier who might by virtue of respect, love, and devotion have made you forget the claims of this foreigner, alike unworthy to be our king and to be your husband."

The queen heaved a heavy sigh.

"When did you lose your skill to read my heart?" she cried. "Must I actually tell you that this love is making me wretched? True, at the very first this unsanctioned love was a keen joy: a new life seemed to wake within my heart; I was drawn on, fascinated by the prayers, the tears, and the despair of this man, by the opportunities that his mother so easily granted, she whom I had always looked upon as my own mother; I have loved him.... O my God, I am still so young, and my past is so unhappy. At times strange thoughts come into my mind: I fancy he no longer loves me, that he never did love me; I fancy he has been led on by ambition, by self-interest, by some ignoble motive, and has only feigned a feeling that he has never really felt. I feel myself a coldness I cannot account for; in his presence I am constrained, I am troubled by his look, his voice makes me tremble: I fear him;

I would sacrifice a year of my life could I never have listened to him."

These words seemed to touch the young confidante to the very depths of her soul; a shade of sadness crossed her brow, her eyelids dropped, and for some time she answered nothing, showing sorrow rather than surprise. Then, lifting her head gently, she said, with visible embarrassment—

"I should never have dared to pass so severe a judgment upon a man whom my sovereign lady has raised above other men by casting upon him a look of kindness; but if Robert of Cabane has deserved the reproach of inconstancy and ingratitude, if he has perjured himself like a coward, he must indeed be the basest of all miserable beings, despising a happiness which other men might have entreated of God the whole time of their life and paid for through eternity. One man I know, who weeps both night and day without hope or consolation, consumed by a slow and painful malady, when one word might yet avail to save him, did it come from the lips of my noble mistress."

"I will not hear another word," cried Joan, suddenly rising; "there shall be no new cause for remorse in my life. Trouble has come upon me through my loves, both lawful and criminal; alas! no longer will I try to control my awful fate, I will bow my head without a murmur. I am the queen, and I must yield myself up for the good of my subjects."

"Will you forbid me, madam," replied Dona Cancha in a kind, affectionate tone—"will you forbid me to name Bertrand of Artois in your presence, that unhappy man, with the beauty of an angel and the modesty of a girl? Now that you are queen and have the life and death of your subjects in your own keeping, will you feel no kindness towards an unfortunate one whose only fault is to adore you, who strives with all his mind and strength to bear a chance look of yours without dying of his joy?"

"I have struggled hard never to look on him," cried the queen, urged by an impulse she was not strong enough to conquer: then, to efface the impression that might well have been made on her friend's mind, she added severely, "I forbid you to pronounce his name before me; and if he should ever venture to complain, I bid you tell him from me that the first time I even suspect the cause of his distress he will be banished for ever from my presence."

"Ah, madam, dismiss me also; for I shall never be strong enough to do so hard a bidding: the unhappy man who cannot awake in your heart so much as a feeling of pity may now be struck down by yourself in your wrath, for here he stands; he has heard your sentence, and come to die at your feet."

The last words were spoken in a louder voice, so that they might be heard from outside, and Bertrand of Artois came hurriedly into the room and fell on his knees before the queen. For a long time past the young lady-in-waiting had perceived that Robert of Cabane had, through his own fault, lost the love of Joan; for his tyranny had indeed become more unendurable to her than her husband's.

Dona Cancha had been quick enough to perceive that

the eyes of her young mistress were wont to rest with a kind of melancholy gentleness on Bertrand, a young man of handsome appearance but with a sad and dreamy expression; so when she made up her mind to speak in his interests, she was persuaded that the queen already loved him. Still, a bright colour overspread Joan's face, and her anger would have fallen on both culprits alike, when in the next room a sound of steps was heard, and the voice of the grand seneschal's widow in conversation with her son fell on the ears of the three young people like a clap of thunder. Dona Cancha, pale as death, stood trembling; Bertrand felt that he was lost—all the more because his presence compromised the queen; Joan only, with that wonderful presence of mind she was destined to preserve in the most difficult crises of her future life, thrust the young man against the carved back of her bed, and concealed him completely beneath the ample curtain: she then signed to Cancha to go forward and meet the governess and her son.

But before we conduct into the queen's room these two persons, whom our readers may remember in Joan's train about the bed of King Robert, we must relate the circumstances which had caused the family of the Catanese to rise with incredible rapidity from the lowest class of the people to the highest rank at court. When Dona Violante of Aragon, first wife of Robert of Anjou, became the mother of Charles, who was later on the Duke of Calabria, a nurse was sought for the infant among the most handsome women of the people. After inspecting many women of equal merit as regards beauty, youth and health, the princess's choice lighted on Philippa, a young Catanese woman, the wife of a fisherman of Trapani, and by condition a laundress. This young woman, as she washed her linen on the bank of a stream, had dreamed strange dreams: she had fancied herself summoned to court, wedded to a great personage, and receiving the honours of a great lady. Thus when she was called to Castel Nuovo her joy was great, for she felt that her dreams now began to be realised. Philippa was installed at the court, and a few months after she began to nurse the child the fisherman was dead and she was a widow. Meanwhile Raymond of Cabane, the major-domo of King Charles II's house, had bought a negro from some corsairs, and having had him baptized by his own name, had given him his liberty; afterwards observing that he was able and intelligent, he had appointed him head cook in the king's kitchen; and then he had gone away to the war. During the absence of his patron the negro managed his own affairs at the court so cleverly, that in a short time he was able to buy land, houses, farms, silver plate, and horses, and could vie in riches with the best in the kingdom; and as he constantly won higher favour in the royal family, he passed on from the kitchen to the wardrobe. The Catanese had also deserved very well of her employers, and as a reward for the care she had bestowed on the child, the princess married her to the negro, and he, as a wedding gift, was granted the title of knight.

From this day forward, Raymond of Cabane and Philippa the laundress rose in the world so rapidly that they had no equal in influence at court. After the death of Dona Violante, the Catanese became the intimate friend of Dona Sandra, Robert's second wife, whom we introduced to our readers at the beginning of this narrative. Charles, her foster son, loved her as a mother, and she was the confidante of his two wives in turn, especially of the second wife, Marie of Valois. And as the quondam laundress had in the end learned all the manners and customs of the court, she was chosen at the birth of Joan and her sister to be governess and mistress over the young girls, and at this juncture Raymond was created major-domo. Finally, Marie of Valois on her deathbed commended the two young princesses to her care, begging her to look on them as her own-daughters. Thus Philippa the Catanese, honoured in future as foster mother of the heiress to the throne of Naples, had power to nominate her husband grand seneschal, one of the seven most important offices in the kingdom, and to obtain knighthood for her sons. Raymond of Cabane was buried like a king in a marble tomb in the church of the Holy Sacrament, and there was speedily joined by two of his sons. The third, Robert, a youth of extraordinary strength and beauty, gave up an ecclesiastical career, and was himself made major-domo, his two sisters being married to the Count of Merlizzi and the Count of Morcone respectively. This was now the state of affairs, and the influence of the grand seneschal's widow seemed for ever established, when an unexpected event suddenly occurred, causing such injury as might well suffice to upset the edifice of her fortunes that had been raised stone by stone patiently and slowly: this edifice was now undermined and threatened to fall in a single day. It was the sudden apparition of Friar Robert, who followed to the court of Rome his young pupil, who from infancy had been Joan's destined husband, which thus shattered all the designs of the Catanese and seriously menaced her future. The monk had not been slow to understand that so long as she remained at the court, Andre would be no more than the slave, possibly even the victim, of his wife. Thus all Friar Robert's thoughts were obstinately concentrated on a single end, that of getting rid of the Catanese or neutralising her influence. The prince's tutor and the governess of the heiress had but to exchange one glance, icy, penetrating, plain to read: their looks met like lightning flashes of hatred and of vengeance. The Catanese, who felt she was detected, lacked courage to fight this man in the open, and so conceived the hope of strengthening her tottering empire by the arts of corruption and debauchery. She instilled by degrees into her pupil's mind the poison of vice, inflamed her youthful imagination with precocious desires, sowed in her heart the seeds of an unconquerable aversion for her husband, surrounded the poor child with abandoned women, and especially attached to her the beautiful and attractive Dona Cancha, who is branded by contemporary authors with the name of a courtesan; then summed up all these lessons in infamy by prostituting Joan to her own son. The poor girl, polluted by sin before she knew what life was, threw her whole self into this first passion with all the ardour of youth, and loved Robert of Cabane so violently, so madly, that the Catanese congratulated herself on the success of her infamy, believing that she held her prey so fast in her toils that her victim would never attempt to escape them.

A year passed by before Joan, conquered by her infatuation, conceived the smallest suspicion of her lover's sincerity. He, more ambitious than affectionate, found it easy to conceal his coldness under the cloak of a brotherly intimacy, of blind submission, and of unswerving devotion; perhaps he would have deceived his mistress for a longer time had not Bertrand of Artois fallen madly in love with Joan. Suddenly the bandage fell from the young girl's eyes; comparing the two with the natural instinct of a woman beloved which never goes astray, she perceived that Robert of Cabane loved her for his own sake, while Bertrand of Artois would give his life to make her happy. A light fell upon her past: she mentally recalled the circumstances that preceded and accompanied her earliest love; and a shudder went through her at the thought that she had been sacrificed to a cowardly seducer by the very woman she had loved most in the world, whom she had called by the name of mother.

Joan drew back into herself, and wept bitterly. Wounded by a single blow in all her affections, at first her grief absorbed her; then, roused to sudden anger, she proudly raised her head, for now her love was changed to scorn. Robert, amazed at her cold and haughty reception of him, following on so great a love, was stung by jealousy and wounded pride. He broke out into bitter reproach and violent recrimination, and, letting fall the mask, once for all lost his place in Joan's heart.

His mother at last saw that it was time to interfere: she rebuked her son, accusing him of upsetting all her plans by his clumsiness.

"As you have failed to conquer her by love," she said, "you must now subdue her by fear. The secret of her honour is in our hands, and she will never dare to rebel. She plainly loves Bertrand of Artois, whose languishing eyes and humble sighs contrast in a striking manner with your haughty indifference and your masterful ways. The mother of the Princes of Tarentum, the Empress of Constantinople, will easily seize an occasion of helping on the princess's love so as to alienate her more and more from her husband: Cancha will be the go between, and sooner or later we shall find Bertrand at Joan's feet. Then she will be able to refuse us nothing."

While all this was going on, the old king died, and the Catanese, who had unceasingly kept on the watch for the moment she had so plainly foreseen, loudly called to her son, when she saw Bertrand slip into Joan's apartment, saying as she drew him after her—

"Follow me, the queen is ours."

It was thus that she and her son came to be there. Joan, standing in the middle of the chamber, pallid, her eyes fixed on the curtains of the bed, concealed her agitation with a smile, and took one step forward towards her governess, stooping to receive the kiss which the latter bestowed upon her every morning. The Catanese embraced her with affected cordiality, and turning, to her son, who had knelt upon one knee, said, pointing to Robert—

"My fair queen, allow the humblest of your subjects to offer his sincere congratulations and to lay his homage at your feet."

"Rise, Robert," said Joan, extending her hand kindly, and with no show of bitterness. "We were brought up together, and I shall never forget that in our childhood—I mean those happy days when we were both innocent—I called you my brother."

"As you allow me, madam," said Robert, with an ironical smile, "I too shall always remember the names you formerly gave me."

"And I," said the Catanese, "shall forget that I speak to the Queen of Naples, in embracing once more my beloved daughter. Come, madam, away with care: you have wept long enough; we have long respected your grief. It is now time to show yourself to these good Neapolitans who bless Heaven continually for granting them a queen so beautiful and good; it is time that your favours fall upon the heads of your faithful subjects, and my son, who surpasses all in his fidelity, comes first to ask a favour of you, in order that he may serve you yet more zealously."

Joan cast on Robert a withering look, and, speaking to the Catanese, said with a scornful air—

"You know, madam, I can refuse your son nothing."

"All he asks," continued the lady, "is a title which is his due, and which he inherited from his father—the title of Grand Seneschal of the Two Sicilies: I trust, my daughter, you will have no difficulty in granting this."

"But I must consult the council of regency."

"The council will hasten to ratify the queen's wishes," replied Robert, handing her the parchment with an imperious gesture: "you need only speak to the Count of Artois."

And he cast a threatening glance at the curtain, which had slightly moved.

"You are right," said the queen at once; and going up to a table she signed the parchment with a trembling hand.

"Now, my daughter, I have come in the name of all the care I bestowed on your infancy, of all the maternal love I have lavished on you, to implore a favour that my family will remember for evermore."

The queen recoiled one step, crimson with astonishment and rage; but before she could find words to reply, the lady continued in a voice that betrayed no feeling—

"I request you to make my son Count of Eboli."

"That has nothing to do with me, madam; the barons of this kingdom would revolt to a man if I were on my own authority to exalt to one of the first dignities the son of a——"

"A laundress and a negro; you would say, madam?" said Robert, with a sneer. "Bertrand of Artois would be annoyed perhaps if I had a title like his."

He advanced a step towards the bed, his hand upon the hilt of his sword.

"Have mercy, Robert!" cried the queen, checking him: "I will do all you ask."

And she signed the parchment naming him Count of Eboli.

"And now," Robert went on impudently, "to show that my new title is not illusory, while you are busy about signing documents, let me have the privilege of taking part in the councils of the crown: make a declaration that, subject to your good pleasure, my mother and I are to have a deliberative voice in the council whenever an important matter is under discussion."

"Never!" cried Joan, turning pale. "Philippa and Robert, you abuse my weakness and treat your queen shamefully. In the last few days I have wept and suffered continually, overcome by a terrible grief; I have no strength to turn to business now. Leave me, I beg: I feel my strength gives way."

"What, my daughter," cried the Catanese hypocritically, "are you feeling unwell? Come and lie down at once." And hurrying to the bed, she took hold of the curtain that concealed the Count of Artois.

The queen uttered a piercing cry, and threw herself before Philippa with the fury of a lioness. "Stop!" she cried in a choking voice; "take the privilege you ask, and now, if you value your own life, leave me."

The Catanese and her son departed instantly, not even waiting to reply, for they had got all they wanted; while Joan, trembling, ran desperately up to Bertrand, who had angrily drawn his dagger, and would have fallen upon the two favourites to take vengeance for the insults they had offered to the queen; but he was very soon disarmed by the lovely shining eyes raised to him in supplication, the two arms cast about him, and the tears shed by Joan: he fell at her feet and kissed them rapturously, with no thought of seeking excuse for his presence, with no word of love, for it was as if they had loved always: he lavished the tenderest caresses on her, dried her tears, and pressed his trembling lips upon her lovely head. Joan began to forget her anger, her vows, and her repentance: soothed by the music of her lover's speech, she returned uncomprehending monosyllables: her heart beat till it felt like breaking, and once more she was falling beneath love's resistless spell, when a new interruption occurred, shaking her roughly out of her ecstasy; but this time the young count was able to pass quietly and calmly into a room adjoining, and Joan prepared to receive her importunate visitor with severe and frigid dignity.

The individual who arrived at so inopportune a moment was little calculated to smooth Joan's ruffled brow, being Charles, the eldest son of the Durazzo family. After he had introduced his fair cousin to the people as their only legitimate sovereign, he had sought on various occasions to obtain an interview with her, which in all probability would be decisive. Charles was one of those men who to gain their end recoil at nothing; devoured by raging ambition and accustomed from his earliest years to conceal his most ardent desires beneath a mask of careless indifference, he marched ever onward, plot succeeding plot, towards the object he was bent upon securing, and never deviated one hair's-breadth from the path he had marked out, but only acted with double prudence after each victory, and with double courage after each defeat. His cheek grew pale with joy; when he hated most, he smiled; in all the emotions of his life, however strong, he was inscrutable. He had sworn to sit on the throne of Naples, and long had believed himself the rightful heir, as being nearest of kin to Robert of all his nephews. To him the hand of Joan would have been given, had not the old king in his latter days conceived the plan of bringing Andre from Hungary and re-establishing the elder branch in his person, though that had long since been forgotten. But his resolution had never for a moment been weakened by the arrival of Andre in the kingdom, or by the profound indifference wherewith Joan, preoccupied with other passion, had always received the advances of her cousin Charles of Durazzo. Neither the love of a woman nor the life of a man was of any account to him when a crown was weighed in the other scale of the balance.

During the whole time that the queen had remained invisible, Charles had hung about her apartments, and now came into her presence with respectful eagerness to inquire for his cousin's health. The young duke had been at pains to set off his noble features and elegant figure by a magnificent dress covered with golden fleur-de-lys and glittering with precious stones. His doublet of scarlet velvet and cap of the same showed up, by their own splendour, the warm colouring of his skin, while his face seemed illumined by his black eyes that shone keen as an eagle's.

Charles spoke long with his cousin of the people's enthusiasm on her accession and of the brilliant destiny before her; he drew a hasty but truthful sketch of the state of the kingdom; and while he lavished praises on the queen's wisdom, he cleverly pointed out what reforms were most urgently needed by the country; he contrived to put so much warmth, yet so much reserve, into his speech that he destroyed the disagreeable impression his arrival had produced. In spite of the irregularities of her youth and the depravity brought about by her wretched education, Joan's nature impelled her to noble action: when the welfare of her subjects was concerned, she rose above the limitations of her age and sex, and, forgetting her strange position, listened to the Duke of Durazzo with the liveliest interest and the kindliest attention. He then hazarded allusions to the dangers that beset a young queen, spoke vaguely of the difficulty in distinguishing between true devotion and cowardly complaisance or interested attachment; he spoke of the ingratitude of many who had been loaded with benefits, and had been most completely trusted. Joan, who had just learned the truth of his words by sad experience, replied with a sigh, and after a moment's silence added—

"May God, whom I call to witness for the loyalty and uprightness of my intentions, may God unmask all traitors and show me my true friends! I know that the burden laid upon me is heavy, and I presume not on my strength, but I trust that the tried experience of those counsellors to whom my uncle entrusted me, the support of my family, and your warm and sincere friendship above all, my dear cousin, will help me to accomplish my duty."

"My sincerest prayer is that you may succeed, my fair

cousin, and I will not darken with doubts and fears a time that ought to be given up to joy; I will not mingle with the shouts of gladness that rise on all sides to proclaim you queen, any vain regrets over that blind fortune which has placed beside the woman whom we all alike adore, whose single glance would make a man more blest than the angels, a foreigner unworthy of your love and unworthy of your throne."

"You forget, Charles," said the queen, putting out her hand as though to check his words, "Andre is my husband, and it was my grandfather's will that he should reign with me."

"Never!" cried the duke indignantly; "he King of Naples! Nay, dream that the town is shaken to its very foundations, that the people rise as one man, that our church bells sound a new Sicilian vespers, before the people of Naples will endure the rule of a handful of wild Hungarian drunkards, a deformed canting monk, a prince detested by them even as you are beloved!"

"But why is Andre blamed? What has he done?"

"What has he done? Why is he blamed, madam? The people blame him as stupid, coarse, a savage; the nobles blame him for ignoring their privileges and openly supporting men of obscure birth; and I, madam,"—here he lowered his voice, "I blame him for making you unhappy."

Joan shuddered as though a wound had been touched by an unkind hand; but hiding her emotion beneath an appearance of calm, she replied in a voice of perfect indifference—

"You must be dreaming, Charles; who has given you leave

to suppose I am unhappy?"

"Do not try to excuse him, my dear cousin," replied Charles eagerly; "you will injure yourself without saving him."

The queen looked fixedly at her cousin, as though she would read him through and through and find out the meaning of his words; but as she could not give credence to the horrible thought that crossed her mind, she assumed a complete confidence in her cousin's friendship, with a view to discovering his plans, and said carelessly—

"Well, Charles, suppose I am not happy, what remedy could you offer me that I might escape my lot?"

"You ask me that, my dear cousin? Are not all remedies good when you suffer, and when you wish for revenge?"

"One must fly to those means that are possible. Andre will not readily give up his pretensions: he has a party of his own, and in case of open rupture his brother the King of Hungary may declare war upon us, and bring ruin and desolation upon our kingdom."

The Duke of Duras faintly smiled, and his countenance assumed a sinister expression.

"You do not understand me," he said.

"Then explain without circumlocution," said the queen, trying to conceal the convulsive shudder that ran through her limbs.

"Listen, Joan," said Charles, taking his cousin's hand and laying it upon his heart: "can you feel that dagger?"

"I can," said Joan, and she turned pale.

"One word from you—and—"

"Yes?"

"To-morrow you will be free."

"A murder!" cried Joan, recoiling in horror: "then I was not deceived; it is a murder that you have proposed."

"It is a necessity," said the duke calmly: "today I advise; later on you will give your orders."

"Enough, wretch! I cannot tell if you are more cowardly or more rash: cowardly, because you reveal a criminal plot feeling sure that I shall never denounce you; rash, because in revealing it to me you cannot tell what witnesses are near to hear it all."

"In any case, madam, since I have put myself in your hands, you must perceive that I cannot leave you till I know if I must look upon myself as your friend or as your enemy."

"Leave me," cried Joan, with a disdainful gesture; "you insult your queen."

"You forget, my dear cousin, that some day I may very likely have a claim to your kingdom."

"Do not force me to have you turned out of this room," said Joan, advancing towards the door.

"Now do not get excited, my fair cousin; I am going: but at least remember that I offered you my hand and you refused it. Remember what I say at this solemn moment: to-day I am the guilty man; some day perhaps I may be the judge."

He went away slowly, twice turning his head, repeating in the language of signs his menacing prophecy. Joan hid her face in her hands, and for a long time remained plunged in dismal reflections; then anger got the better of all her other feelings, and she summoned Dona Cancha, bidding her not to allow anybody to enter, on any pretext whatsoever.

This prohibition was not for the Count of Artois, for the reader will remember that he was in the adjoining room.

CHAPTER III

Night fell, and from the Molo to the Mergellina, from the Capuano Castle to the hill of St. Elmo, deep silence had succeeded the myriad sounds that go up from the noisiest city in the world. Charles of Durazzo, quickly walking away from the square of the Correggi, first casting one last look of vengeance at the Castel Nuovo, plunged into the labyrinth of dark streets that twist and turn, cross and recross one another, in this ancient city, and after a quarter of an hour's walking, that was first slow, then very rapid, arrived at his ducal palace near the church of San Giovanni al Mare. He gave certain instructions in a harsh, peremptory tone to a page who took his sword and cloak. Then Charles shut himself into his room, without going up to see his poor mother, who was weeping, sad and solitary over her son's ingratitude, and like every other mother taking her revenge by praying God to bless him.

The Duke of Durazzo walked up and down his room several times like a lion in a cage, counting the minutes in a fever of impatience, and was on the point of summoning a servant and renewing his commands, when two dull raps on the door informed him that the person he was waiting for had arrived. He opened at once, and a man of about fifty, dressed in black from head to foot, entered, humbly bowing, and carefully shut the door behind him. Charles threw himself into an easy-chair, and gazing fixedly at the man who stood before him, his eyes on the ground and his arms crossed upon his breast in an attitude of the deepest respect and blind obedience, he said slowly, as though weighing each word—

"Master Nicholas of Melazzo, have you any remembrance left of the services I once rendered you?"

The man to whom these words were addressed trembled in every limb, as if he heard the voice of Satan come to claim his soul; then lifting a look of terror to his questioner's face, he asked in a voice of gloom—

"What have I done, my lord, to deserve this reproach?"

"It is not a reproach: I ask a simple question."

"Can my lord doubt for a moment of my eternal gratitude? Can I forget the favours your Excellency showed me? Even if I could so lose my reason and my memory, are not my wife and son ever here to remind me that to you we owe all our life, our honour, and our fortune? I was guilty of an infamous act," said the notary, lowering his voice, "a crime that would not only have brought upon my head the penalty of death, but which meant the confiscation of my goods, the ruin of my family, poverty and shame for my only son—that very son, sire, for whom I, miserable wretch, had wished to ensure a brilliant future by means of my frightful crime: you had in your hands the proofs of this!"

"I have them still."

"And you will not ruin me, my lord," resumed the notary, trembling; "I am at your feet, your Excellency; take my life and I will die in torment without a murmur, but save my son since you have been so merciful as to spare him till now; have pity on his mother; my lord, have pity!"

"Be assured," said Charles, signing to him to rise; "it is nothing to do with your life; that will come later, perhaps. What I wish to ask of you now is a much simpler, easier matter."

"My lord, I await your command."

"First," said the duke, in a voice of playful irony, "you must draw up a formal contract of my marriage."

"At once, your Excellency."

"You are to write in the first article that my wife brings me as dowry the county of Alba, the jurisdiction of Grati and Giordano, with all castles, fiefs, and lands dependent thereto."

"But, my lord—" replied the poor notary, greatly embarrassed.

"Do you find any difficulty, Master Nicholas?"

"God forbid, your Excellency, but—"

"Well, what is it?"

"Because, if my lord will permit, because there is only one person in Naples who possesses that dowry your Excellency mentions."

"And so?"

"And she," stammered the notary, embarrassed more and more, "—she is the queen's sister."

"And in the contract you will write the name of Marie of Anjou."

"But the young maiden," replied Nicholas timidly, "whom your Excellency would marry is destined, I thought, under the will of our late king of blessed memory, to become the wife of the King of Hungary or else of the grandson of the King of France."

"Ah, I understand your surprise: you may learn from this that an uncle's intentions are not always the same as his nephew's."

"In that case, sire, if I dared—if my lord would deign to give me leave—if I had an opinion I might give, I would humbly entreat your Excellency to reflect that this would mean the abduction of a minor."

"Since when did you learn to be scrupulous, Master Nicholas?"

These words were uttered with a glance so terrible that the poor notary was crushed, and had hardly the strength to reply—

"In an hour the contract will be ready."

"Good: we agree as to the first point," continued Charles, resuming his natural tone of voice. "You now will hear my second charge. You have known the Duke of Calabria's valet for the last two years pretty intimately?"

"Tommaso Pace; why, he is my best friend."

"Excellent. Listen, and remember that on your discretion the safety or ruin of your family depends. A plot will soon be on foot against the queen's husband; the conspirators no doubt will gain over Andre's valet, the man you call your best friend; never leave him for an instant, try to be his shadow; day by day and hour by hour come to me and report the progress of the plot, the names of the plotters."

"Is this all your Excellency's command?"

"All."

The notary respectfully bowed, and withdrew to put the orders at once into execution. Charles spent the rest of that night writing to his uncle the Cardinal de Perigord, one of the most influential prelates at the court of Avignon. He begged him before all things to use his authority so as to prevent Pope Clement from signing the bull that would sanction Andre's coronation, and he ended his letter by earnestly entreating his uncle to win the pope's consent to his marriage with the queen's sister.

"We shall see, fair cousin," he said as he sealed his letter, "which of us is best at understanding where our interest lies. You would not have me as a friend, so you shall have me as an enemy. Sleep on in the arms of your lover: I will wake you when the time comes. I shall be Duke of Calabria perhaps some day, and that title, as you well know, belongs to the heir to the throne."

The next day and on the following days a remarkable change took place in the behaviour of Charles towards Andre: he showed him signs of great friendliness, cleverly flattering his inclinations, and even persuading Friar Robert that, far from feeling any hostility in the matter of Andre's coronation, his most earnest desire was that his uncle's wishes should be respected; and that, though he might have given the impression of acting contrary to them, it had only been done with a view to appeasing the populace, who in their first excitement might have been stirred up to insurrection against the Hungarians. He declared with much warmth that he heartily detested the people about the queen, whose counsels tended to lead her astray, and he promised to join Friar Robert in the endeavour to get rid of Joan's favourites by all such means as fortune might put at his disposal. Although the Dominican did not believe in the least in the sincerity of his ally's protestations, he yet gladly welcomed the aid which might prove so useful to the prince's cause, and attributed the sudden change of front to some recent rupture between Charles and his cousin, promising himself that he would make capital out of his resentment. Be that as it might, Charles wormed himself into Andre's heart, and after a few days one of them could hardly be seen without the other. If Andre went out hunting, his greatest pleasure in life, Charles was eager to put his pack or his falcons at his disposal; if Andre rode through the town, Charles was always ambling by his side. He gave way to his whims, urged him to extravagances, and inflamed his angry passions: in a word, he was the good angel—or the bad one—who inspired his every thought and guided his every action.

Joan soon understood this business, and as a fact had expected it. She could have ruined Charles with a single word; but she scorned so base a revenge, and treated him with utter contempt. Thus the court was split into two factions: the Hungarians with Friar Robert at their head and supported by Charles of Durazzo; on the other side all the nobility of Naples, led by the Princes of Tarentum. Joan, influenced by the grand seneschal's widow and her two daughters, the

Countesses of Terlizzi and Morcone, and also by Dona Cancha and the Empress of Constantinople, took the side of the Neapolitan party against the pretensions of her husband. The partisans of the queen made it their first care to have her name inscribed upon all public acts without adding Andre's; but Joan, led by an instinct of right and justice amid all the corruption of her court, had only consented to this last after she had taken counsel with Andre d'Isernia, a very learned lawyer of the day, respected as much for his lofty character as for his great learning. The prince, annoyed at being shut out in this way, began to act in a violent and despotic manner. On his own authority he released prisoners; he showered favours upon Hungarians, and gave especial honours and rich gifts to Giovanni Pipino, Count of Altanuera, the enemy of all others most dreaded and detested by the Neapolitan barons. Then the Counts of San Severino, Mileto, Terlizzi and Balzo, Calanzaro and Sant' Angelo, and most of the grandees, exasperated by the haughty insolence of Andre's favourite, which grew every day more outrageous, decided that he must perish, and his master with him, should he persist in attacking their privileges and defying their anger.

Moreover, the women who were about Joan at the court egged her on, each one urged by a private interest, in the pursuit of her fresh passion. Poor Joan,—neglected by her husband and betrayed by Robert of Cabane— gave way beneath the burden of duties beyond her strength to bear, and fled for refuge to the arms of Bertrand of Artois, whose love she did not even attempt to resist; for every feeling for religion and virtue had been destroyed in her own set purpose, and her young inclinations had been early bent towards vice, just as the bodies of wretched children are bent and their bones broken by jugglers when they train them. Bertrand himself felt an adoration for her surpassing ordinary human passion. When he reached the summit of a happiness to which in his wildest dreams he had never dared to aspire, the young count nearly lost his reason. In vain had his father, Charles of Artois (who was Count of Aire, a direct descendant of Philip the Bold, and one of the regents of the kingdom), attempted by severe admonitions to stop him while yet on the brink of the precipice: Bertrand would listen to nothing but his love for Joan and his implacable hatred for all the queen's enemies. Many a time, at the close of day, as the breeze from Posilippo or Sorrento coming from far away was playing in his hair, might Bertrand be seen leaning from one of the casements of Castel Nuovo, pale and motionless, gazing fixedly from his side of the square to where the Duke of Calabria and the Duke of Durazzo came galloping home from their evening ride side by side in a cloud of dust. Then the brows of the young count were violently contracted, a savage, sinister look shone in his blue eyes once so innocent, like lightning a thought of death and vengeance flashed into his mind; he would all at once begin to tremble, as a light hand was laid upon his shoulder; he would turn softly, fearing lest the divine apparition should vanish to the skies; but there beside him stood a young girl, with cheeks aflame and heaving breast, with brilliant liquid eyes: she had come to tell how her past day had been spent, and to offer her forehead for the kiss that should reward her labours and unwilling absence. This woman, dictator of laws and administrator of justice among grave magistrates and stern ministers, was but fifteen years old; this man, who knew her griefs, and to avenge them was meditating regicide, was not yet twenty: two children of earth, the playthings of an awful destiny!

Two months and a few days after the old king's death, on the morning of Friday the 28th of March of the same year, 1343, the widow of the grand seneschal, Philippa, who, had already contrived to get forgiven for the shameful trick she had used to secure all her son's wishes, entered the queen's apartments, excited by a genuine fear, pale and distracted, the bearer of news that spread terror and lamentation throughout the court: Marie, the queen's younger sister, had disappeared.

The gardens and outside courts had been searched for any trace of her; every corner of the castle had been examined; the guards had been threatened with torture, so as to drag the truth from them; no one had seen anything of the princess, and nothing could be found that suggested either flight or abduction. Joan, struck down by this new blow in the midst of other troubles, was for a time utterly prostrated; then, when she had recovered from her first surprise, she behaved as all people do if despair takes the place of reason: she gave orders for what was already done to be done again, she asked the same questions that could only bring the same answers, and poured forth vain regrets and unjust reproaches. The news spread through the town, causing the greatest astonishment: there arose a great commotion in the castle, and the members of the regency hastily assembled, while couriers were sent out in every direction, charged to promise 12,000 ducats to whomsoever should discover the place where the princess was concealed. Proceedings were at once taken against the soldiers who were on guard at the fortress at the time of the disappearance.

Bertrand of Artois drew the queen apart, telling her his suspicions, which fell directly upon Charles of Durazzo; but Joan lost no time in persuading him of the improbability of his hypothesis: first of all, Charles had never once set his foot in Castel Nuovo since the day of his stormy interview with the queen, but had made a point of always leaving Andre by the bridge when he came to the town with him; besides, it had never been noticed, even in the past, that the young duke had spoken to Marie or exchanged looks with her: the result of all attainable evidence was that no stranger had entered the castle the evening before except a notary named Master Nicholas of Melazzo, an old person, half silly, half fanatical, for whom Tommaso Pace, valet de chambre to the Duke of Calabria, was ready to answer with his life. Bertrand yielded to the queen's reasoning, and day by day advanced new suggestions, each less probable than the last, to draw his mistress on to feel a hope that he was far from feeling himself.

But a month later, and precisely on the morning of Monday the 30th of April, a strange and unexpected scene took place, an exhibition of boldness transcending all calculations. The Neapolitan people were stupefied in astonishment, and the grief of Joan and her friends was changed to indignation. Just as the clock of San Giovanni struck twelve, the gate of the magnificent palace of the Durazzo flung open its folding doors, and there came forth to the sound of trumpets a double file of cavaliers on richly caparisoned horses, with the duke's arms on their shields. They took up their station round the house to prevent the people outside from disturbing a ceremony which was to take place before the eyes of an immense crowd, assembled suddenly, as by a miracle, upon the square. At the back of the court stood an altar, and upon the steps lay two crimson velvet cushions embroidered with the fleur-de-lys of France and the ducal crown. Charles came forward, clad in a dazzling dress, and holding by the hand the queen's sister, the Princess Marie, at that time almost thirteen years of age. She knelt down timidly on one of the cushions, and when Charles had done the same, the grand almoner of the Duras house asked the young duke solemnly what was his intention in appearing thus humbly before a minister of the Church. At these words Master Nicholas of Melazzo took his place on the left of the altar, and read in a firm, clear voice, first, the contract of marriage between Charles and Marie, and then the apostolic letters from His Holiness the sovereign pontiff, Clement VI, who in his own name removing all obstacles that might impede the union, such as the age of the young bride and the degrees of affinity between the two parties, authorised his dearly beloved son

Charles, Duke of Durazzo and Albania, to take in marriage the most illustrious Marie of Anjou, sister of Joan, Queen of Naples and Jerusalem, and bestowed his benediction on the pair.

The almoner then took the young girl's hand, and placing it in that of Charles, pronounced the prayers of the Church. Charles, turning half round to the people, said in a loud voice—

"Before God and man, this woman is my wife."

"And this man is my husband," said Marie, trembling.

"Long live the Duke and Duchess of Durazzo!" cried the crowd, clapping their hands. And the young pair, at once mounting two beautiful horses and followed by their cavaliers and pages, solemnly paraded through the town, and re-entered their palace to the sound of trumpets and cheering.

When this incredible news was brought to the queen, her first feeling was joy at the recovery of her sister; and when Bertrand of Artois was eager to head a band of barons and cavaliers and bent on falling upon the cortege to punish the traitor, Joan put up her hand to stop him with a very mournful look.

"Alas!" she said sadly, "it is too late. They are legally married, for the head of the Church—who is moreover by my grandfather's will the head of our family—has granted his permission. I only pity my poor sister; I pity her for becoming so young the prey of a wretched man who sacrifices her to his own ambition, hoping by this marriage to establish a claim to the throne. O God! what a strange fate oppresses the royal house of Anjou! My father's early death in the midst of his triumphs; my mother's so quickly after; my sister and I, the sole offspring of Charles I, both before we are women grown fallen into the hands of cowardly men, who use us but as the stepping-stones of their ambition!" Joan fell back exhausted on her chair, a burning tear trembling on her eyelid.

"This is the second time," said Bertrand reproachfully, "that I have drawn my sword to avenge an insult offered to you, the second time I return it by your orders to the scabbard. But remember, Joan, the third time will not find me so docile, and then it will not be Robert of Cabane or Charles of Durazzo that I shall strike, but him who is the cause of all your misfortunes."

"Have mercy, Bertrand! do not you also speak these words; whenever this horrible thought takes hold of me, let me come to you: this threat of bloodshed that is drummed into my ears, this sinister vision that haunts my sight; let me come to you, beloved, and weep upon your bosom, beneath your breath cool my burning fancies, from your eyes draw some little courage to revive my perishing soul. Come, I am quite unhappy enough without needing to poison the future by an endless remorse. Tell me rather to forgive and to forget, speak not of hatred and revenge; show me one ray of hope amid the darkness that surrounds me; hold up my wavering feet, and push me not into the abyss."

Such altercations as this were repeated as often as any fresh wrong arose from the side of Andre or his party; and in proportion as the attacks made by Bertrand and his friends gained in vehemence—and we must add, in justice—so did Joan's objections weaken. The Hungarian rule, as it became more and more arbitrary and unbearable, irritated men's minds to such a point that the people murmured in secret and the nobles proclaimed aloud their discontent. Andre's soldiers indulged in a libertinage which would have been intolerable in a conquered city: they were found everywhere brawling in the taverns or rolling about disgustingly drunk in the gutters; and the prince, far from rebuking such orgies, was accused of sharing them himself. His former tutor, who ought to have felt bound to drag him away from so ignoble a mode of life, rather strove to immerse him in degrading pleasures, so as to keep him out of business matters; without suspecting it, he was hurrying on the denouement of the terrible drama that was being acted behind the scenes at Castel Nuovo. Robert's widow, Dona Sancha of Aragon, the good and sainted lady whom our readers may possibly have forgotten, as her family had done, seeing that God's anger was hanging over her house, and that no counsels, no tears or prayers of hers could avail to arrest it, after wearing mourning for her husband one whole year, according to her promise, had taken the veil at the convent of Santa Maria delta Croce, and deserted the court and its follies and passions, just as the prophets of old, turning their back on some accursed city, would shake the dust from off their sandals and depart. Sandra's retreat was a sad omen, and soon the family dissensions, long with difficulty suppressed, sprang forth to open view; the storm that had been threatening from afar broke suddenly over the town, and the thunderbolt was shortly to follow.

On the last day of August 1344, Joan rendered homage to Americ, Cardinal of Saint Martin and legate of Clement VI, who looked upon the kingdom of Naples as being a fief of the Church ever since the time when his predecessors had presented it to Charles of Anjou, and overthrown and excommunicated the house of Suabia. For this solemn ceremony the church of Saint Clara was chosen, the burial-place of Neapolitan kings, and but lately the tomb of the grandfather and father of the young queen, who reposed to right and left of the high altar. Joan, clad in the royal robe, with the crown upon her head, uttered her oath of fidelity between the hands of the apostolic legate in the presence of her husband, who stood behind her simply as a witness, just like the other princes of the blood. Among the prelates with their pontifical insignia who formed the brilliant following of the envoy, there stood the Archbishops of Pisa, Bari, Capua, and Brindisi, and the reverend fathers Ugolino, Bishop of Castella, and Philip, Bishop of Cavaillon, chancellor to the queen. All the nobility of Naples and Hungary were present at this ceremony, which debarred Andre from the throne in a fashion at once formal and striking. Thus, when they left the church the excited feelings of both parties made a crisis imminent, and such hostile glances, such threatening words were exchanged, that the prince, finding himself too weak to contend against his enemies, wrote the same evening to his mother, telling her that he was about to leave a country where from his infancy upwards he had experienced nothing but deceit and disaster.

Those who know a mother's heart will easily guess that Elizabeth of Poland was no sooner aware of the danger that threatened her son than she travelled to Naples, arriving there before her coming was suspected. Rumour spread abroad that the Queen of Hungary had come to take her son away with her, and the unexpected event gave rise to strange comments: the fever of excitement now blazed up in another direction. The Empress of Constantinople, the Catanese, her two daughters, and all the courtiers, whose calculations were upset by Andre's departure, hurried to honour the arrival of the Queen of Hungary by offering a very cordial and respectful reception, with a view to showing her that, in the midst of a court so attentive and devoted, any isolation or bitterness of feeling on the young prince's part must spring from his pride, from an unwarrantable mistrust, and his naturally savage and untrained character. Joan received her husband's mother with so much proper dignity in her behaviour that, in spite of preconceived notions, Elizabeth could not help admiring the noble seriousness and earnest feeling she saw in her daughter-in-law. To make the visit more pleasant to an honoured guest, fetes and tournaments were given, the barons vying with one another in display of wealth and luxury. The Empress of Constantinople, the Catanese, Charles of Duras and his young wife, all paid the utmost attention to the mother of the prince. Marie, who by reason of her extreme youth and gentleness of character had no share in any intrigues, was guided quite as much by her natural feeling as by her husband's orders when she offered to the Queen of Hungary those marks of regard and affection that she might have felt for her own mother. In spite, however, of these protestations of respect and love, Elizabeth of Poland trembled for her son, and, obeying a maternal instinct, chose to abide by her original intention, believing that she should never feel safe until Andre was far away from a court in appearance so friendly but in reality so treacherous. The person who seemed most disturbed by the departure, and tried to hinder it by every means in his power, was Friar Robert. Immersed in his political schemes, bending over his mysterious plans with all the eagerness of a gambler who is on the point of gaining, the Dominican, who thought himself on the eve of a tremendous event, who by cunning, patience, and labour hoped to scatter his enemies and to reign as absolute autocrat, now falling suddenly from the edifice of his dream, stiffened himself by a mighty effort to stand and resist the mother of his pupil. But fear cried too loud in the heart of Elizabeth for all the reasonings of the monk to lull it to rest: to every argument he advanced she simply said that while her son was not king and had not entire unlimited power, it was imprudent to leave him exposed to his enemies. The monk, seeing that all was indeed lost and that he could not contend against the fears of this woman, asked only the boon of three days' grace, at the end of which time, should a reply he was expecting have not arrived, he said he would not only give up his opposition to

Andre's departure, but would follow himself, renouncing for ever a scheme to which he had sacrificed everything.

Towards the end of the third day, as Elizabeth was definitely making her preparations for departure, the monk entered radiant. Showing her a letter which he had just hastily broken open, he cried triumphantly—

"God be praised, madam! I can at last give you incontestable proofs of my active zeal and accurate foresight."

Andre's mother, after rapidly running through the document, turned her eyes on the monk with yet some traces of mistrust in her manner, not venturing to give way to her sudden joy.

"Yes, madam," said the monk, raising his head, his plain features lighted up by his glance of intelligence—"yes, madam, you will believe your eyes, perhaps, though you would never believe my words: this is not the dream of an active imagination, the hallucination of a credulous mind, the prejudice of a limited intellect; it is a plan slowly conceived, painfully worked out, my daily thought and my whole life's work. I have never ignored the fact that at the court of Avignon your son had powerful enemies; but I knew also that on the very day I undertook a certain solemn engagement in the prince's name, an engagement to withdraw those laws that had caused coldness between the pope and Robert; who was in general so devoted to the Church, I knew very well that my offer would never be rejected, and this argument of mine I kept back for the last. See, madam, my calculations are correct; your enemies are put to shame and your son is triumphant."

Then turning to Andre, who was just coming in and stood dumbfounded at the threshold on hearing the last words, he added—

"Come, my son, our prayers are at last fulfilled: you are king."

"King!" repeated Andre, transfixed with joy, doubt, and amazement.

"King of Sicily and Jerusalem: yes, my lord; there is no need for you to read this document that brings the joyful, unexpected news. You can see it in your mother's tears; she holds out her arms to press you to her bosom; you can see it in the happiness of your old teacher; he falls on his knees at your feet to salute you by this title, which he would have paid for with his own blood had it been denied to you much longer."

"And yet," said Elizabeth, after a moment's mournful reflection, "if I obey my presentiments, your news will make no difference to our plans for departure."

"Nay, mother," said Andre firmly, "you would not force me to quit the country to the detriment of my honour. If I have made you feel some of the bitterness and sorrow that have spoiled my own young days because of my cowardly enemies, it is not from a poor spirit, but because I was powerless, and knew it, to take any sort of striking vengeance for their secret insults, their crafty injuries, their underhand intrigues. It was not because my arm wanted strength, but because my head wanted a crown. I might have put an end to some of these wretched beings, the least dangerous maybe; but it would have been striking in the dark; the ringleaders would have escaped, and I should never have really got to the bottom of their infernal plots. So I have silently eaten out my own heart in shame and indignation. Now that my sacred rights are recognised by the Church, you will see, my mother, how these terrible barons, the queen's counsellors, the governors of the kingdom, will lower their heads in the dust: for they are threatened with no sword and no struggle; no peer of their own is he who speaks, but the king; it is by him they are accused, by the law they shall be condemned, and shall suffer on the scaffold."

"O my beloved son," cried the queen in tears, "I never doubted your noble feelings or the justice of your claims; but when your life is in danger, to what voice can I listen but the voice of fear? what can move my counsels but the promptings of love?"

"Mother, believe me, if the hands and hearts alike of these cowards had not trembled, you would have lost your son long ago."

"It is not violence that I fear, my son, it is treachery."

"My life, like every man's, belongs to God, and the lowest of sbirri may take it as I turn the corner of the street; but a king owes something to his people."

The poor mother long tried to bend the resolution of Andre by reason and entreaties; but when she had spoken her last word and shed her last tear, she summoned Bertram de Baux, chief-justice of the kingdom, and Marie, Duchess of Durazzo. Trusting in the old man's wisdom and the girl's innocence, she commended her son to them in the tenderest and most affecting words; then drawing from her own hand a ring richly wrought, and taking the prince aside, she slipped it upon his finger, saying in a voice that trembled with emotion as she pressed him to her heart—

"My son, as you refuse to come with me, here is a wonderful talisman, which I would not use before the last extremity. So long as you wear this ring on your finger, neither sword nor poison will have power against you."

"You see then, mother," said the prince, smiling, "with this protection there is no reason at all to fear for my life."

"There are other dangers than sword or poison," sighed the queen.

"Be calm, mother: the best of all talismans is your prayer to God for me: it is the tender thought of you that will keep me for ever in the path of duty and justice; your maternal love will watch over me from afar, and cover me like the wings of a guardian angel."

Elizabeth sobbed as she embraced her son, and when she left him she felt her heart was breaking. At last she made up her mind to go, and was escorted by the whole court, who had never changed towards her for a moment in their chivalrous and respectful devotion. The poor mother, pale, trembling, and faint, leaned heavily upon Andre's arm, lest she should fall. On the ship that was to take her for ever from her son, she cast her arms for the last time about his neck, and there hung a long time, speechless, tearless, and motionless; when the signal for departure was given, her women took her in their arms half swooning. Andre stood on the shore with the feeling of death at his heart: his eyes were fixed upon the sail that carried ever farther from him the only being he loved in the world. Suddenly he fancied he beheld something white moving a long way off: his mother had recovered her senses by a great effort, and had dragged herself up to the bridge to give a last signal of farewell: the unhappy lady knew too well that she would never see her son again.

At almost the same moment that Andre's mother left the kingdom, the former queen of Naples, Robert's widow, Dona Sancha, breathed her last sigh. She was buried in the convent of Santa Maria delta Croce, under the name of Clara, which she had assumed on taking her vows as a nun, as her epitaph tells us, as follows:

"Here lies, an example of great humility, the body of the sainted sister Clara, of illustrious memory, otherwise Sancha, Queen of Sicily and Jerusalem, widow of the most serene Robert, King of Jerusalem and Sicily, who, after the death of the king her husband, when she had completed a year of widowhood, exchanged goods temporary for goods eternal. Adopting for the love of God a voluntary poverty, and distributing her goods to the poor, she took upon her the rule of obedience in this celebrated convent of Santa Croce, the work of her own hands, in the year 1344, on the gist of January of the twelfth indiction, where, living a life of holiness under the rule of the blessed Francis, father of the poor, she ended her days religiously in the year of our Lord

1345, on the 28th of July of the thirteenth indiction. On the day following she was buried in this tomb."

The death of Dona Sancha served to hasten on the catastrophe which was to stain the throne of Naples with blood: one might almost fancy that God wished to spare this angel of love and resignation the sight of so terrible a spectacle, that she offered herself as a propitiatory sacrifice to redeem the crimes of her family.

CHAPTER IV

Eight days after the funeral of the old queen, Bertrand of Artois came to Joan, distraught, dishevelled, in a state of agitation and confusion impossible to describe.

Joan went quickly up to her lover, asking him with a look of fear to explain the cause of his distress.

"I told you, madam," cried the young baron excitedly, "you will end by ruining us all, as you will never take any advice from me."

"For God's sake, Bertrand, speak plainly: what has happened? What advice have I neglected?"

"Madam, your noble husband, Andre of Hungary, has just been made King of Jerusalem and Sicily, and acknowledged by the court of Avignon, so henceforth you will be no better than his slave."

"Count of Artois, you are dreaming."

"No, madam, I am not dreaming: I have this fact to prove the truth of my words, that the pope's ambassadors are arrived at Capua with the bull for his coronation, and if they do not enter Castel Nuovo this very evening, the delay is only to give the new king time to make his preparations."

The queen bent her head as if a thunderbolt had fallen at her feet.

"When I told you before," said the count, with growing fury, "that we ought to use force to make a stand against him, that we ought to break the yoke of this infamous tyranny and get rid of the man before he had the means of hurting you, you always drew back in childish fear, with a woman's cowardly hesitation."

Joan turned a tearful look upon her lover.

"God, my God!" she cried, clasping her hands in desperation, "am I to hear for ever this awful cry of death! You too, Bertrand, you too say the word, like Robert of Cabane, like Charles of Duras? Wretched man, why would you raise this bloody spectre between us, to check with icy hand our adulterous kisses? Enough of such crimes; if his wretched ambition makes him long to reign, let him be king: what matters his power to me, if he leaves me with your love?"

"It is not so sure that our love will last much longer."

"What is this, Bertrand? You rejoice in this merciless torture."

"I tell you, madam, that the King of Naples has a black flag ready, and on the day of his coronation it will be carried before him."

"And you believe," said Joan, pale as a corpse in its shroud, "—you believe that this flag is a threat?"

"Ay, and the threat begins to be put in execution."

The queen staggered, and leaned against a table to save herself from falling.

"Tell me all," she cried in a choking voice; "fear not to shock me; see, I am not trembling. O Bertrand, I entreat you!"

"The traitors have begun with the man you most esteemed, the wisest counsellor of the crown, the best of magistrates, the noblest-hearted, most rigidly virtuous——"

"Andrea of Isernia!"

"Madam, he is no more."

Joan uttered a cry, as though the noble old man had been slain before her eyes: she respected him as a father; then, sinking back, she remained profoundly silent.

"How did they kill him?" she asked at last, fixing her great eyes in terror on the count.

"Yesterday evening, as he left this castle, on the way to his own home, a man suddenly sprang out upon him before the Porta Petruccia: it was one of Andre's favourites, Conrad of Gottis chosen no doubt because he had a grievance against the incorruptible magistrate on account of some sentence passed against him, and the murder would therefore be put down to motives of private revenge. The cowardly wretch gave a sign to two or three companions, who surrounded the victim and robbed him of all means of escape. The poor old man looked fixedly at his assassin, and asked him what he wanted. 'I want you to lose your life at my hands, as I lost my case at yours!' cried the murderer, and leaving him no time to answer, he ran him through with his sword. Then the rest fell upon the poor man, who did not even try to call for help, and his body was riddled with wounds and horribly mutilated, and then left bathed in its blood."

"Terrible!" murmured the queen, covering her face.

"It was only their first effort; the proscription lists are already full: Andre must needs have blood to celebrate his accession to the throne of Naples. And do you know, Joan, whose name stands first in the doomed list?"

"Whose?" cried the queen, shuddering from head to foot.

"Mine," said the count calmly.

"Yours!" cried Joan, drawing herself up to her full height; "are you to be killed next! Oh, be careful, Andre; you have pronounced your own death-sentence. Long have I turned aside the dagger pointing to your breast, but you put an end to all my patience. Woe to you, Prince of Hungary! the blood which you have spilt shall fall on your own head."

As she spoke she had lost her pallor; her lovely face was fired with revenge, her eyes flashed lightning. This child of sixteen was terrible to behold; she pressed her lover's hand with convulsive tenderness, and clung to him as if she would screen him with her own body.

"Your anger is awakened too late," said he gently and sadly; for at this moment Joan seemed so lovely that he could reproach her with nothing. "You do not know that his mother has left him a talisman preserving him from sword and poison?"

"He will die," said Joan firmly; the smile that lighted up her face was so unnatural that the count was dismayed, and dropped his eyes.

The next day the young Queen of Naples, lovelier, more smiling than ever, sitting carelessly in a graceful attitude beside a window which looked out on the magnificent view of the bay, was busy weaving a cord of silk and gold. The sun had run nearly two-thirds of his fiery course, and was gradually sinking his rays in the clear blue waters where Posilippo's head is reflected with its green and flowery crown.

A warm, balmy breeze that had passed over the orange trees of Sorrento and Amalfi felt deliciously refreshing to the inhabitants of the capital, who had succumbed to torpor in the enervating softness of the day. The whole town was waking from a long siesta, breathing freely after a sleepy interval; the Molo was covered with a crowd of eager people dressed out in the brightest colours; the many cries of a festival, joyous songs, love ditties sounded from all quarters of the vast amphitheatre, which is one of the chief marvels of creation; they came to the ears of Joan, and she listened as she bent over her work, absorbed in deep thought. Suddenly, when she seemed most busily occupied, the indefinable feeling of someone near at hand, and the touch of something on her shoulder, made her start: she turned as though waked from a dream by contact with a serpent, and perceived her husband, magnificently dressed, carelessly leaning against the back of her chair. For a long time past the prince had not come to his wife in this familiar fashion, and to the queen the pretence of affection and careless behaviour augured ill. Andre did not appear to notice the look of hatred and terror that had escaped Joan in spite of herself, and assuming the best expression of gentleness as that his straight hard features could contrive to put on in such circumstances as these, he smilingly asked—

"Why are you making this pretty cord, dear dutiful wife?"

"To hang you with, my lord," replied the queen, with a smile.

Andre shrugged his shoulders, seeing in the threat so

incredibly rash nothing more than a pleasantry in rather bad taste. But when he saw that Joan resumed her work, he tried to renew the conversation.

"I admit," he said, in a perfectly calm voice, "that my question is quite unnecessary: from your eagerness to finish this handsome piece of work, I ought to suspect that it is destined for some fine knight of yours whom you propose to send on a dangerous enterprise wearing your colours. If so, my fair queen, I claim to receive my orders from your lips: appoint the time and place for the trial, and I am sure beforehand of carrying off a prize that I shall dispute with all your adorers."

"That is not so certain," said Joan, "if you are as valiant in war as in love." And she cast on her husband a look at once seductive and scornful, beneath which the young man blushed up to his eyes.

"I hope," said Andre, repressing his feelings, "I hope soon to give you such proofs of my affection that you will never doubt it again."

"And what makes you fancy that, my lord?"

"I would tell you, if you would listen seriously."

"I am listening."

"Well, it is a dream I had last night that gives me such confidence in the future."

"A dream! You surely ought to explain that."

"I dreamed that there was a grand fete in the town: an immense crowd filled the streets like an overflowing torrent, and the heavens were ringing with their shouts of joy; the gloomy granite facades were hidden by hangings of silk and festoons of flowers; the churches were decorated as though for some grand ceremony. I was riding side by side with you." Joan made a haughty movement: "Forgive me, madam, it was only a dream: I was on your right, riding a fine white horse, magnificently caparisoned, and the chief-justice of the kingdom carried before me a flag unfolded in sign of honour. After riding in triumph through the main thoroughfares of the city, we arrived, to the sound of trumpets and clarions, at the royal church of Saint Clara, where your grandfather and my uncle are buried, and there, before the high altar, the pope's ambassador laid your hand in mine and pronounced a long discourse, and then on our two heads in turn placed the crown of Jerusalem and Sicily; after which the nobles and the people shouted in one voice, 'Long live the King and Queen of Naples!' And I, wishing to perpetuate the memory of so glorious a day, proceeded to create knights among the most zealous in our court."

"And do you not remember the names of the chosen persons whom you judged worthy of your royal favours?"

"Assuredly, madam: Bertrand, Count of Artois."

"Enough, my lord; I excuse you from naming the rest: I always supposed you were loyal and generous, but you give me fresh proof of it by showing favour to men whom I most honour and trust. I cannot tell if your wishes are likely soon to be realised, but in any case feel sure of my perpetual gratitude."

Joan's voice did not betray the slightest emotion; her

look had became kind, and the sweetest smile was on her lips. But in her heart Andre's death was from that moment decided upon. The prince, too much preoccupied with his own projects of vengeance, and too confident in his all-powerful talisman and his personal valour, had no suspicion that his plans could be anticipated. He conversed a long time with his wife in a chatting, friendly way, trying to spy out her secret, and exposing his own by his interrupted phrases and mysterious reserves. When he fancied that every cloud of former resentment, even the lightest, had disappeared from Joan's brow, he begged her to go with her suite on a magnificent hunting expedition that he was organising for the 20th of August, adding that such a kindness on her part would be for him a sure pledge of their reconciliation and complete forgetfulness of the past. Joan promised with a charming grace, and the prince retired fully satisfied with the interview, carrying with him the conviction that he had only to threaten to strike a blow at the queen's favourite to ensure her obedience, perhaps even her love.

But on the eve of the 20th of August a strange and terrible scene was being enacted in the basement storey of one of the lateral towers of Castel Nuovo. Charles of Durazzo, who had never ceased to brood secretly over his infernal plans, had been informed by the notary whom he had charged to spy upon the conspirators, that on that particular evening they were about to hold a decisive meeting, and therefore, wrapped in a black cloak, he glided into the underground corridor and hid himself behind a pillar, there to await the issue of the conference. After two dreadful hours of suspense, every second marked out by the beating of his heart, Charles fancied he heard the sound of a door very carefully opened; the feeble ray of a lantern in the vault scarcely served to dispel the darkness, but a man coming away from the wall approached him walking like a living statue. Charles gave a slight cough, the sign agreed upon. The man put out his light and hid away the dagger he had drawn in case of a surprise.

"Is it you, Master Nicholas?" asked the duke in a low voice.

"It is I, my lord."

"What is it?"

"They have just fixed the prince's death for tomorrow, on his way to the hunt."

"Did you recognise every conspirator?"

"Every one, though their faces were masked; when they gave their vote for death, I knew them by their voices."

"Could you point out to me who they are?"

"Yes, this very minute; they are going to pass along at the end of this corridor. And see, here is Tommaso Pace walking in front of them to light their way."

Indeed, a tall spectral figure, black from head to foot, his face carefully hidden under a velvet mask, walked at the end of the corridor, lamp in hand, and stopped at the first step of a staircase which led to the upper floors. The conspirators advanced slowly, two by two, like a procession of ghosts, appeared for one moment in the circle of light made by the torch, and again disappeared into shadow.

"See, there are Charles and Bertrand of Artois," said the notary; "there are the Counts of Terlizzi and Catanzaro; the grand admiral and grand seneschal, Godfrey of Marsan, Count of Squillace, and Robert of Cabane, Count of Eboli; the two women talking in a low voice with the eager gesticulations are Catherine of Tarentum, Empress of Constantinople, and Philippa the Catanese, the queen's governess and chief lady; there is Dona Cancha, chamberwoman and confidante of Joan; and there is the Countess of Morcone."

The notary stopped on beholding a shadow alone, its head bowed, with arms hanging loosely, choking back her sobs beneath a hood of black.

"Who is the woman who seems to drag herself so painfully along in their train?" asked the duke, pressing his companion's arm.

"That woman," said the notary, "is the queen." "Ah, now I see," thought Charles, breathing freely, with the same sort of satisfaction that Satan no doubt feels when a long coveted soul falls at length into his power.

"And now, my lord," continued Master Nicholas, when all had returned once more into silence and darkness, "if you have bidden me spy on these conspirators with a view to saving the young prince you are protecting with love and vigilance, you must hurry forward, for to-morrow maybe it will be too late."

"Follow me," cried the duke imperiously; "it is time you should know my real intention, and then carry out my orders with scrupulous exactness."

With these words he drew him aside to a place opposite to where the conspirators had just disappeared. The notary mechanically followed through a labyrinth of dark corridors and secret staircases, quite at a loss how to account for the sudden change that had come over his master—crossing one of the ante-chambers in the castle, they came upon Andre, who joyfully accosted them; grasping the hand of his cousin Duras in his affectionate manner, he asked him in a pressing way that would brook no refusal, "Will you be of our hunting party to-morrow, duke?"

"Excuse me, my lord," said Charles, bowing down to the ground; "it will be impossible for me to go to-morrow, for my wife is very unwell; but I entreat you to accept the best falcon I have."

And here he cast upon the notary a petrifying glance.

The morning of the 20th of August was fine and calm—the irony of nature contrasting cruelly with the fate of mankind. From break of day masters and valets, pages and knights, princes and courtiers, all were on foot; cries of joy were heard on every side when the queen arrived on a snow-white horse, at the head of the young and brilliant throng. Joan was perhaps paler than usual, but that might be because she had been obliged to rise very early. Andre, mounted on one of the most fiery of all the steeds he had tamed, galloped beside his wife, noble and proud, happy in his own powers, his youth, and the thousand gilded hopes that a brilliant future seemed to offer. Never had the court of Naples shown so brave an aspect: every feeling of distrust and hatred seemed entirely forgotten; Friar Robert himself, suspicious as he was by nature, when he saw the joyous cavalcade go by under his window, looked out with pride, and stroking his beard, laughed at his own seriousness.

Andre's intention was to spend several days hunting between Capua and Aversa, and only to return to Naples when all was in readiness for his coronation. Thus the first day they hunted round about Melito, and went through two or three villages in the land of Labore. Towards evening the court stopped at Aversa, with a view to passing the night there, and since at that period there was no castle in the place worthy of entertaining the queen with her husband and numerous court, the convent of St. Peter's at Majella was converted into a royal residence: this convent had been built by Charles II in the year of our Lord 1309.

While the grand seneschal was giving orders for supper and the preparation of a room for Andre and his wife, the prince, who during the whole day had abandoned himself entirely to his favourite amusement, went up on the terrace to enjoy the evening air, accompanied by the good Isolda, his beloved nurse, who loved him more even than his mother, and would not leave his side for a moment. Never had the prince appeared so animated and happy: he was in ecstasies over the beauty of the country, the clear air, the scent of the trees around; he besieged his nurse with a thousand queries, never waiting for an answer; and they were indeed long in coming, for poor Isolda was gazing upon him with that appearance of fascination which makes a mother absent-minded when her child is talking: Andre was eagerly telling her about a terrible boar he had chased that morning across the woods, how it had lain foaming at his feet, and Isolda interrupted him to say he had a grain of dust in his eye. Then Andre was full of his plans for the future, and Isolda stroked his fair hair, remarking that he must be feeling very tired. Then, heeding nothing but his own joy and excitement, the young prince hurled defiance at destiny, calling by all his gods on dangers to come forward, so that he might have the chance of quelling them, and the poor nurse exclaimed, in a flood of tears, "My child, you love me no longer."

Out of all patience with these constant interruptions, Andre scolded her kindly enough, and mocked at her childish fears. Then, paying no attention to a sort of melancholy that was coming over him, he bade her tell him old tales of his childhood, and had a long talk about his brother Louis, his absent mother, and tears were in his eyes when he recalled her last farewell. Isolda listened joyfully, and answered all he asked; but no fell presentiment shook her heart: the poor woman loved Andre with all the strength of her soul; for him she would have given up her life in this world and in the world to come; yet she was not his mother.

When all was ready, Robert of Cabane came to tell the prince that the queen awaited him; Andre cast one last look at the smiling fields beneath the starry heavens, pressed his nurse's hand to his lips and to his heart, and followed the grand seneschal slowly and, it seemed, with some regret. But soon the brilliant lights of the room, the wine that circulated freely, the gay talk, the eager recitals of that day's exploits served to disperse the cloud of gloom that had for a moment overspread the countenance of the prince. The queen alone, leaning on the table with fixed eyes and lips that never moved, sat at this strange feast pale and cold as a baleful ghost summoned from the tomb to disturb the joy of the party. Andre, whose brain began to be affected by the draughts of wine from Capri and Syracuse, was annoyed at his wife's look, and attributing it to contempt, filled a goblet to the brim and presented it to the queen. Joan visibly trembled, her lips moved convulsively; but the conspirators drowned in their noisy talk the involuntary groan that escaped her. In the midst of a general uproar, Robert of Cabane proposed that they should serve generous supplies of the same wine drunk at the royal table to the Hungarian guards who were keeping watch at the approaches to the convent, and this liberality evoked frenzied applause. The shouting of the soldiers soon gave witness to their gratitude for the unexpected gift, and mingled with the hilarious toasts of the banqueters. To put the finishing touch to Andre's excitement, there were cries on every side of "Long live the Queen! Long live His Majesty the King of Naples!"

The orgy lasted far into the night: the pleasures of the next day were discussed with enthusiasm, and Bertrand of Artois protested in a loud voice that if they were so late now some would not rise early on the morrow. Andre declared that, for his part, an hour or two's rest would be enough to get over his fatigue, and he eagerly protested that it would be well for others to follow his example. The Count of Terlizzi seemed to express some doubt as to the prince's punctuality. Andre insisted, and challenging all the barons present to see who would be up first, he retired with the queen to the room that had been reserved for them, where he very soon fell into a deep and heavy sleep. About two o'clock in the morning, Tommaso Pace, the prince's valet and first usher of the royal apartments, knocked at his master's door to rouse him for the chase. At the first knock, all was silence; at the second, Joan, who had not closed her eyes all night, moved as if to rouse her husband and warn him of the threatened danger; but at the third knock the unfortunate young man suddenly awoke, and hearing in the next room sounds of laughter and whispering, fancied that they were making a joke of his laziness, and jumped out of bed bareheaded, in nothing but his shirt, his shoes half on and half off. He opened the door; and at this point we translate literally the account of Domenico Gravina, a historian of much esteem. As soon as the prince appeared, the conspirators all at once fell upon him, to strangle him with their hands; believing he could not die by poison or sword, because of the charmed ring given him by his poor mother. But Andre was so strong and active, that when he perceived the infamous treason he defended himself with more than human strength, and with dreadful cries got free from his murderers, his face all bloody, his fair hair pulled out in handfuls. The unhappy young man tried to gain his own bedroom, so as to get some weapon and valiantly resist the assassins; but as he reached the door, Nicholas of

Melazzo, putting his dagger like a bolt into the lock, stopped his entrance. The prince, calling aloud the whole time and imploring the protection of his friends, returned to the hall; but all the doors were shut, and no one held out a helping hand; for the queen was silent, showing no uneasiness about her husband's death.

But the nurse Isolda, terrified by the shouting of her beloved son and lord, leapt from her bed and went to the window, filling the house with dreadful cries. The traitors, alarmed by the mighty uproar, although the place was lonely and so far from the centre of the town that nobody could have come to see what the noise was, were on the point of letting their victim go, when Bertrand of Artois, who felt he was more guilty than the others, seized the prince with hellish fury round the waist, and after a desperate struggle got him down; then dragging him by the hair of his head to a balcony which gave upon the garden, and pressing one knee upon his chest, cried out to the others—

"Come here, barons: I have what we want to strangle him with."

And round his neck he passed a long cord of silk and gold, while the wretched man struggled all he could. Bertrand quickly drew up the knot, and the others threw the body over the parapet of the balcony, leaving it hanging between earth and sky until death ensued. When the Count of Terlizzi averted his eyes from the horrid spectacle, Robert of Cabane cried out imperiously—

"What are you doing there? The cord is long enough for

us all to hold: we want not witnesses, we want accomplices!"

As soon as the last convulsive movements of the dying man had ceased, they let the corpse drop the whole height of the three storeys, and opening the doors of the hall, departed as though nothing had happened.

Isolda, when at last she contrived to get a light, rapidly ran to the queen's chamber, and finding the door shut on the inside, began to call loudly on her Andre. There was no answer, though the queen was in the room. The poor nurse, distracted, trembling, desperate, ran down all the corridors, knocked at all the cells and woke the monks one by one, begging them to help her look for the prince. The monks said that they had indeed heard a noise, but thinking it was a quarrel between soldiers drunken perhaps or mutinous, they had not thought it their business to interfere. Isolda eagerly, entreated: the alarm spread through the convent; the monks followed the nurse, who went on before with a torch. She entered the garden, saw something white upon the grass, advanced trembling, gave one piercing cry, and fell backward.

The wretched Andre was lying in his blood, a cord round his neck as though he were a thief, his head crushed in by the height from which he fell. Then two monks went upstairs to the queen's room, and respectfully knocking at the door, asked in sepulchral tones—

"Madam, what would you have us do with your husband's corpse?"

And when the queen made no answer, they went down again slowly to the garden, and kneeling one at the head, the other at the foot of the dead man, they began to recite penitential psalms in a low voice. When they had spent an hour in prayer, two other monks went up in the same way to Joan's chamber, repeating the same question and getting no answer, whereupon they relieved the first two, and began themselves to pray. Next a third couple went to the door of this inexorable room, and coming away perturbed by their want of success, perceived that there was a disturbance of people outside the convent, while vengeful cries were heard amongst the indignant crowd. The groups became more and more thronged, threatening voices were raised, a torrent of invaders threatened the royal dwelling, when the queen's guard appeared, lance in readiness, and a litter closely shut, surrounded by the principal barons of the court, passed through the crowd, which stood stupidly gazing. Joan, wrapped in a black veil, went back to Castel Nuovo, amid her escort; and nobody, say the historians, had the courage to say a word about this terrible deed.

CHAPTER V

The terrible part that Charles of Durazzo was to play began as soon as this crime was accomplished. The duke left the corpse two whole days exposed to the wind and the rain, unburied and dishonoured, the corpse of a man whom the pope had made King of Sicily and Jerusalem, so that the indignation of the mob might be increased by the dreadful sight. On the third he ordered it to be conveyed with the utmost pomp to the cathedral of Naples, and assembling all the Hungarians around the catafalque, he thus addressed them, in a voice of thunder:—

"Nobles and commoners, behold our king hanged like a dog by infamous traitors. God will soon make known to us the names of all the guilty: let those who desire that justice may be done hold up their hands and swear against murderers bloody persecution, implacable hatred, everlasting vengeance."

It was this one man's cry that brought death and desolation to the murderers' hearts, and the people dispersed about the town, shrieking, "Vengeance, vengeance!"

Divine justice, which knows naught of privilege and respects no crown, struck Joan first of all in her love. When the two lovers first met, both were seized alike with terror and disgust; they recoiled trembling, the queen seeing in Bertrand her husband's executioner, and he in her the cause of his crime, possibly of his speedy punishment. Bertrand's looks were disordered, his cheeks hollow, his eyes encircled with black rings, his mouth horribly distorted; his arm and forefinger extended towards his accomplice, he seemed to behold a frightful vision rising before him. The same cord he had used when he strangled Andre, he now saw round the queen's neck, so tight that it made its way into her flesh: an invisible force, a Satanic impulse, urged him to strangle with his own hands the woman he had loved so dearly, had at one time adored on his knees. The count rushed out of the room with gestures of desperation, muttering incoherent words; and as he shewed plain signs of mental aberration, his father, Charles of Artois, took him away, and they went that same evening to their palace of St. Agatha, and there prepared a defence in case they should be attacked.

But Joan's punishment, which was destined to be slow as well as dreadful, to last thirty-seven years and end in a ghastly death, was now only beginning. All the wretched beings who were stained with Andre's death came in turn to her to demand the price of blood. The Catanese and her son, who held in their hands not only the queen's honour but her life, now became doubly greedy and exacting. Dona Cancha no longer put any bridle on her licentiousness, and the Empress of Constantinople ordered her niece to marry her eldest son, Robert, Prince of Tarentum. Joan, consumed by remorse, full of indignation and shame at the arrogant conduct of her subjects, dared scarcely lift her head, and stooped to entreaties, only stipulating for a few days' delay before giving her answer: the empress consented, on condition that her son should come to reside at Castel Nuovo, with permission to see the queen once a day. Joan bowed her head in silence, and Robert of Tarentum was installed at the castle.

Charles of Durazzo, who by the death of Andre had practically become the head of the family, and, would, by the terms of his grandfather's will, inherit the kingdom by right of his wife Marie in the case of Joan's dying without lawful issue, sent to the queen two commands: first, that she should not dream of contracting a new marriage without first consulting him in the choice of a husband; secondly, that she should invest him at once with the title of Duke of Calabria. To compel his cousin to make these two concessions, he added that if she should be so ill advised as to refuse either of them, he should hand over to justice the proofs of the crime and the names of the murderers. Joan, bending beneath the weight of this new difficulty, could think of no way to avoid it; but Catherine, who alone was stout enough to fight this nephew of hers, insisted that they must strike at the Duke of Durazzo in his ambition and hopes, and tell him, to begin with—what was the fact—that the queen was pregnant. If, in spite of this news, he persisted in his plans, she would find some means or other, she said, of causing trouble and discord in her nephew's family, and wounding him in his most intimate affections or closest interests, by publicly dishonouring him through his wife or his mother.

Charles smiled coldly when his aunt came to tell him from the queen that she was about to bring into the world an infant, Andre's posthumous child. What importance could a babe yet unborn possibly have—as a fact, it lived only a few months—in the eyes of a man who with such admirable coolness got rid of people who stood in his wary, and that moreover by the hand of his own enemies? He told the empress that the happy news she had condescended to bring him in person, far from diminishing his kindness towards his cousin, inspired him rather with more interest and goodwill; that consequently he reiterated his suggestion, and renewed his promise not to seek vengeance for his dear Andre, since in a certain sense the crime was not complete should a child be destined to survive; but in case of a refusal he declared himself inexorable. He cleverly gave Catherine to understand that, as she had some interest herself in the prince's death, she ought for her own sake to persuade the queen to stop legal proceedings.

The empress seemed to be deeply impressed by her nephew's threatening attitude, and promised to do her best to persuade the queen to grant all he asked, on condition, however, that Charles should allow the necessary time for carrying through so delicate a business. But Catherine profited by this delay to think out her own plan of revenge, and ensure the means of certain success. After starting several projects eagerly and then regretfully abandoning them, she fixed upon an infernal and unheard-of scheme, which the mind would refuse to believe but for the unanimous testimony of historians. Poor Agnes of Duras, Charles's mother, had for some few days been suffering with an inexplicable weariness, a slow painful malady with which her son's restlessness and violence may have had not a little to do. The empress resolved that the first effect of her hatred was to fall upon this unhappy mother. She summoned the Count of Terlizzi and Dona Cancha, his mistress, who by the queen's orders had been attending Agnes since her illness began. Catherine suggested to the young chamberwoman, who was at that time with child, that she should deceive the doctor by representing that certain signs of her own condition really belonged to the sick woman, so that he, deceived by the false indications, should be compelled to admit to Charles of Durazzo that his mother was guilty and dishonoured. The Count of Terlizzi, who ever since he had taken part in the regicide trembled in fear of discovery, had nothing to oppose to the empress's desire, and Dona Cancha, whose head was as light as her heart was corrupt, seized with a foolish gaiety on any chance of taking her revenge on the prudery of the only princess of the blood who led a pure life at a court that was renowned for its depravity. Once assured that her accomplices would be prudent and obedient, Catherine began to spread abroad certain vague and dubious but terribly serious rumours, only needing proof, and soon after the cruel accusation was started it was repeated again and again in confidence, until it reached the ears of Charles.

At this amazing revelation the duke was seized with a fit of trembling. He sent instantly for the doctor, and asked imperiously what was the cause of his mother's malady. The doctor turned pale and stammered; but when Charles grew threatening he admitted that he had certain grounds for suspecting that the duchess was enceinte, but as he might easily have been deceived the first time, he would make a second investigation before pronouncing his opinion in so serious a matter. The next day, as the doctor came out of the bedroom, the duke met him, and interrogating him with an agonised gesture, could only judge by the silence that his fears were too well confirmed. But the doctor, with excess of caution, declared that he would make a third trial. Condemned criminals can suffer no worse than Charles in the long hours that passed before that fatal moment when he learned that his mother was indeed guilty. On the third day the doctor stated on his soul and conscience that Agnes of Durazzo was pregnant.

"Very good," said Charles, dismissing the doctor with no sign of emotion.

That evening the duchess took a medicine ordered by the doctor; and when, half an hour later, she was assailed with violent pains, the duke was warned that perhaps other physicians ought to be consulted, as the prescription of the ordinary doctor, instead of bringing about an improvement in her state, had only made her worse.

Charles slowly went up to the duchess's room, and sending away all the people who were standing round her bed, on the pretext that they were clumsy and made his mother worse, he shut the door, and they were alone. Then poor Agnes, forgetting her internal agony when she saw her son, pressed his hand tenderly and smiled through her tears.

Charles, pale beneath his bronzed complexion, his forehead moist with a cold sweat, and his eyes horribly dilated, bent over the sick woman and asked her gloomily—

"Are you a little better, mother?"

"Ah, I am in pain, in frightful pain, my poor Charles. I feel as though I have molten lead in my veins. O my son, call your brothers, so that I may give you all my blessing for the last time, for I cannot hold out long against this pain. I am burning. Mercy! Call a doctor: I know I have been poisoned."

Charles did not stir from the bedside.

"Water!" cried the dying woman in a broken voice,—"water! A doctor, a confessor! My children—I want my children!"

And as the duke paid no heed, but stood moodily silent, the poor mother, prostrated by pain, fancied that grief had robbed her son of all power of speech or movement, and so, by a desperate effort, sat up, and seizing him by the arm, cried with all the strength she could muster—

"Charles, my son, what is it? My poor boy, courage; it is nothing, I hope. But quick, call for help, call a doctor. Ah, you have no idea of what I suffer."

"Your doctor," said Charles slowly and coldly, each word piercing his mother's heart like a dagger,—"your doctor cannot come."

"Oh why?" asked Agnes, stupefied.

"Because no one ought to live who knows the secret of our shame."

"Unhappy man!" she cried, overwhelmed with, pain and terror, "you have murdered him! Perhaps you have poisoned your mother too! Charles, Charles, have mercy on your own soul!"

"It is your doing," said Charles, without show of emotion: "you have driven me into crime and despair; you have caused my dishonour in this world and my damnation in the next."

"What are you saying? My own Charles, have mercy! Do not let me die in this horrible uncertainty; what fatal delusion is blinding you? Speak, my son, speak: I am not feeling the poison now. What have I done? Of what have I been accused?"

She looked with haggard eyes at her son: her maternal love still struggled against the awful thought of matricide; at last, seeing that Charles remained speechless in spite of her entreaties, she repeated, with a piercing cry—

"Speak, in God's name, speak before I die!"

"Mother, you are with child."

"What!" cried Agnes, with a loud cry, which broke her very heart. "O God, forgive him! Charles, your mother forgives and blesses you in death."

Charles fell upon her neck, desperately crying for help: he would now have gladly saved her at the cost of his life, but it was too late. He uttered one cry that came from his heart, and was found stretched out upon his mother's corpse.

Strange comments were made at the court on the death of the Duchess of Durazzo and her doctor's disappearance; but there was no doubt at all that grief and gloom were furrowing wrinkles on Charles's brow, which was already sad enough. Catherine alone knew the terrible cause of her nephew's depression, for to her it was very plain that the duke at one blow had killed his mother and her physician. But she had never expected a reaction so sudden and violent in a man who shrank before no crime. She had thought Charles capable of everything except remorse. His gloomy, self absorbed silence seemed a bad augury for her plans. She had desired to cause trouble for him in his own family, so that he might have no time to oppose the marriage of her son with the queen; but she had shot beyond her mark, and Charles, started thus on the terrible path of crime, had now broken through the bonds of his holiest affections, and gave himself up to his bad passions with feverish ardour and a savage desire for revenge. Then Catherine had recourse to gentleness and submission. She gave her son to understand that there was only one way of obtaining the queen's hand, and that was by flattering the ambition of Charles and in some sort submitting himself to his patronage. Robert of Tarentum understood this, and ceased making court to Joan, who received his devotion with cool kindness, and attached himself closely to Charles, paying him much the same sort of respect and deference that he himself had affected for Andre, when the thought was first in his mind of causing his ruin. But the Duke of Durazzo was by no means deceived as to the devoted friendship shown towards him by the heir of the house of Tarentum, and pretending to be deeply touched by the unexpected change of feeling, he all the time kept a strict guard on Robert's actions.

 An event outside all human foresight occurred to upset the calculations of the two cousins. One day while they were out together on horseback, as they often were since their pretended reconciliation, Louis of Tarentum, Robert's youngest brother, who had always felt for Joan a chivalrous, innocent love,—a love which a young man of twenty is apt to lock up in his heart as a secret treasure,—Louis, we say, who had held aloof from the infamous family conspiracy and had not soiled his hands with Andre's blood, drawn on by an irrepressible passion, all at once appeared at the gates of Castel Nuovo; and while his brother was wasting precious hours in asking for a promise of marriage, had the bridge raised and gave the soldiers strict orders to admit no one. Then, never troubling himself about Charles's anger or Robert's jealousy, he hurried to the queen's room, and there, says Domenico Gravina, without any preamble, the union was consummated.

On returning from his ride, Robert, astonished that the bridge was not at once lowered for him, at first loudly called upon the soldiers on guard at the fortress, threatening severe punishment for their unpardonable negligence; but as the gates did not open and the soldiers made no sign of fear or regret, he fell into a violent fit of rage, and swore he would hang the wretches like dogs for hindering his return home. But the Empress of Constantinople, terrified at the bloody quarrel beginning between the two brothers, went alone and on foot to her son, and making use of her maternal authority to beg him to master his feelings, there in the presence of the crowd that had come up hastily to witness the strange scene, she related in a low voice all that had passed in his absence.

A roar as of a wounded tiger escaped from Robert's breast: all but blind with rage, he nearly trampled his mother under the feet of his horse, which seemed to feel his master's anger, and plunging violently, breathed blood from his nostrils. When the prince had poured every possible execration on his brother's head, he turned and galloped away from the accursed castle, flying to the Duke of Durazzo, whom he had only just left, to tell him of this outrage and stir him to revenge. Charles was talking carelessly with his young wife, who was but little used to such tranquil conversation and expansiveness, when the Prince of Tarentum, exhausted, out of breath, bathed in perspiration, came up with his incredible tale. Charles made him say it twice over, so impossible did Louis's audacious enterprise appear to him. Then quickly changing from doubt to fury, he struck his brow with his iron glove, saying that as the queen defied him he would make her tremble even in her castle and in her lover's arms. He threw one withering look on Marie, who interceded tearfully for her sister, and pressing Robert's hand with warmth, vowed that so long as he lived Louis should never be Joan's husband.

That same evening he shut himself up in his study, and wrote letters whose effect soon appeared. A bull, dated June 2, 1346, was addressed to Bertram de Baux, chief-justice of the kingdom of Sicily and Count of Monte Scaglioso, with orders to make the most strict inquiries concerning Andre's murderers, whom the pope likewise laid under his anathema, and to punish them with the utmost rigour of the law. But a secret note was appended to the bull which was quite at variance with the designs of Charles: the sovereign pontiff expressly bade the chief-justice not to implicate the queen in the proceedings or the princes of the blood, so as to avoid worse disturbances, reserving, as supreme head of the Church and lord of the kingdom, the right of judging them later on, as his wisdom might dictate.

For this imposing trial Bertram de Baux made great preparations. A platform was erected in the great hall of tribunal, and all the officers of the crown and great state dignitaries, and all the chief barons, had a place behind the enclosure where the magistrates sat. Three days after Clement VI's bull had been published in the capital, the chief-justice was ready for a public examination of two accused persons. The two culprits who had first fallen into the hands of justice were, as one may easily suppose, those whose condition was least exalted, whose lives were least valuable, Tommaso Pace and Nicholas of Melazzo. They were led before the tribunal to be first of all tortured, as the custom was. As they approached the judges, the notary passing by Charles in the street had time to say in a low voice—

"My lord, the time has come to give my life for you: I will do my duty; I commend my wife and children to you."

Encouraged by a nod from his patron, he walked on firmly and deliberately. The chief-justice, after establishing the identity of the accused, gave them over to the executioner and his men to be tortured in the public square, so that their sufferings might serve as a show and an example to the crowd. But no sooner was Tommaso Pace tied to the rope, when to the great disappointment of all he declared that he would confess everything, and asked accordingly to be taken back before his judges. At these words, the Count of Terlizzi, who was following every movement of the two men with mortal anxiety, thought it was all over now with him and his accomplices; and so, when Tommaso Pace was turning his steps towards the great hall, led by two guards, his hands tied behind his back, and followed by the notary, he contrived to take him into a secluded house, and squeezing his throat with great force, made him thus put his tongue out, whereupon he cut it off with a sharp razor.

The yells of the poor wretch so cruelly mutilated fell on the ears of the Duke of Durazzo: he found his way into the room where the barbarous act had been committed just as the Count of Terlizzi was coming out, and approached the notary, who had been present at the dreadful spectacle and had not given the least sign of fear or emotion. Master Nicholas, thinking the same fate was in store for him, turned calmly to the duke, saying with a sad smile—

"My lord, the precaution is useless; there is no need for you to cut out my tongue, as the noble count has done to my poor companion. The last scrap of my flesh may be torn off without one word being dragged from my mouth. I have promised, my lord, and you have the life of my wife and the future of my children as guarantee for my word."

"I do not ask for silence," said the duke solemnly; "you can free me from all my enemies at once, and I order you to denounce them at the tribunal."

The notary bowed his head with mournful resignation; then raising it in affright, made one step up to the duke and murmured in a choking voice—

"And the queen?"

"No one would believe you if you ventured to denounce her; but when the Catanese and her son, the Count of Terlizzi and his wife and her most intimate friends, have been accused by you, when they fail to endure the torture, and when they denounce her unanimously—"

"I see, my lord. You do not only want my life; you would have my soul too. Very well; once more I commend to you my children."

With a deep sigh he walked up to the tribunal. The chief-justice asked Tommaso Pace the usual questions, and a shudder of horror passed through the assembly when they saw the poor wretch in desperation opening his mouth, which streamed with blood. But surprise and terror reached their height when Nicholas of Melazzo slowly and firmly gave a list of Andre's murderers, all except the queen and the princes of the blood, and went on to give all details of the assassination.

Proceedings were at once taken for the arrest of the grand seneschal, Robert of Cabane, and the Counts of Terlizzi and Morcone, who were present and had not ventured to make any movement in self-defence. An hour later, Philippa, her two daughters, and Dona Cancha joined them in prison, after vainly imploring the queen's protection. Charles and Bertrand of Artois, shut up in their fortress of Saint Agatha, bade defiance to justice, and several others, among them the Counts of Meleto and Catanzaro, escaped by flight.

As soon as Master Nicholas said he had nothing further to confess, and that he had spoken the whole truth and nothing but the truth, the chief-justice pronounced sentence amid a profound silence; and without delay Tommaso Pace and the notary were tied to the tails of two horses, dragged through the chief streets of the town, and hanged in the market place.

The other prisoners were thrown into a subterranean vault, to be questioned and put to the torture on the following day. In the evening, finding themselves in the same dungeon, they reproached one another, each pretending he had been dragged into the crime by someone else. Then Dona Cancha, whose strange character knew no inconsistencies, even face to face with death and torture, drowned with a great burst of laughter the lamentations of her companions, and joyously exclaimed—

"Look here, friends, why these bitter recriminations—this ill-mannered raving? We have no excuses to make, and we are all equally guilty. I am the youngest of all, and not the ugliest, by your leave, ladies, but if I am condemned, at least I will die cheerfully. For I have never denied myself any pleasure I could get in this world, and I can boast that much will be forgiven me, for I have loved much: of that you, gentlemen, know something. You, bad old man," she continued to the Count of Terlizzi, "do you not remember lying by my side in the queen's ante-chamber? Come, no blushes before your noble family; confess, my lord, that I am with child by your Excellency; and you know how we managed to make up the story of poor Agnes of Durazzo and her pregnancy—God rest her soul! For my part, I never supposed the joke would take such a serious turn all at once. You know all this and much more; spare your lamentations, for, by my word, they are getting very tiresome: let us prepare to die joyously, as we have lived."

With these words she yawned slightly, and, lying down on the straw, fell into a deep sleep, and dreamed as happy dreams as she had ever dreamed in her life.

On the morrow from break of day there was an immense crowd on the sea front. During the night an enormous palisade had been put up to keep the people away far enough for them to see the accused without hearing anything. Charles of Durazzo, at the head of a brilliant cortege of knights and pages, mounted on a magnificent horse, all in black, as a sign of mourning, waited near the enclosure. Ferocious joy shone in his eyes as the accused made their way through the crowd, two by two, their wrists tied with ropes; for the duke every minute expected to hear the queen's name spoken. But the chief-justice, a man of experience, had prevented indiscretion of any kind by fixing a hook in the tongue of each one. The poor creatures were tortured on a ship, so that nobody should hear the terrible confessions their sufferings dragged from them.

But Joan, in spite of the wrongs that most of the conspirators had done her, felt a renewal of pity for the woman she had once respected as a mother, for her childish companions and her friends, and possibly also some remains of love for Robert of Cabane, and sent two messengers to beg Bertram de Baux to show mercy to the culprits. But the chief-justice seized these men and had them tortured; and on their confession that they also were implicated in Andre's murder, he condemned them to the same punishment as the others. Dona Cancha alone, by reason of her situation, escaped the torture, and her sentence was deferred till the day of her confinement.

As this beautiful girl was returning to prison, with many a smile for all the handsomest cavaliers she could see in the crowd, she gave a sign to Charles of Durazzo as she neared him to come forward, and since her tongue had not been pierced (for the same reason) with an iron instrument, she said some words to him a while in a low voice.

Charles turned fearfully pale, and putting his hand to his sword, cried—

"Wretched woman!"

"You forget, my lord, I am under the protection of the law."

"My mother!—oh, my poor mother!" murmured Charles in a choked voice, and he fell backward.

The next morning the people were beforehand with the executioner, loudly demanding their prey. All the national troops and mercenaries that the judicial authorities could command were echelonned in the streets, opposing a sort of dam to the torrent of the raging crowd. The sudden insatiable cruelty that too often degrades human nature had awaked in the populace: all heads were turned with hatred and frenzy; all imaginations inflamed with the passion for revenge; groups of men and women, roaring like wild beasts, threatened to knock down the walls of the prison, if the condemned were not handed over to them to take to the place of punishment: a great murmur arose, continuous, ever the same, like the growling of thunder: the queen's heart was petrified with terror.

But, in spite of the desire of Bertram de Baux to satisfy the popular wish, the preparations for the solemn execution were not completed till midday, when the sun's rays fell scorchingly upon the town. There went up a mighty cry from ten thousand palpitating breasts when a report first ran through the crowd that the prisoners were about to appear. There was a moment of silence, and the prison doors rolled slowly back on their hinges with a rusty, grating noise. A triple row of horsemen, with lowered visor and lance in rest, started the procession, and amid yells and curses the condemned prisoners came out one by one, each tied upon a cart, gagged and naked to the waist, in charge of two executioners, whose orders were to torture them the whole length of their way. On the first cart was the former laundress of Catana, afterwards wife of the grand seneschal and governess to the queen, Philippa of Cabane: the two executioners at right and left of her scourged her with such fury that the blood spurting up from the wounds left a long track in all the streets passed by the cortege.

Immediately following their mother on separate carts came the Countesses of Terlizzi and Morcone, the elder no more than eighteen years of age. The two sisters were so marvellously beautiful that in the crowd a murmur of surprise was heard, and greedy eyes were fixed upon their naked trembling shoulders. But the men charged to torture them gazed with ferocious smiles upon their forms of seductive beauty, and, armed with sharp knives, cut off pieces of their flesh with a deliberate enjoyment and threw them out to the crowd, who eagerly struggled to get them, signing to the executioners to show which part of the victims' bodies they preferred.

Robert of Cabane, the grand seneschal, the Counts of Terlizzi and Morcone, Raymond Pace, brother of the old valet who had been executed the day before, and many more, were dragged on similar carts, and both scourged with ropes and slashed with knives; their flesh was torn out with red-hot pincers, and flung upon brazen chafing-dishes. No cry of pain was heard from the grand seneschal, he never stirred once in his frightful agony; yet the torturers put such fury into their work that the poor wretch was dead before the goal was reached.

In the centre of the square of Saint Eligius an immense stake was set up: there the prisoners were taken, and what was left of their mutilated bodies was thrown into the flames. The Count of Terlizzi and the grand seneschal's widow were still alive, and two tears of blood ran down the cheeks of the miserable mother as she saw her son's corpse and the palpitating remains of her two daughters cast upon the fire—they by their stifled cries showed that they had not ceased to suffer. But suddenly a fearful noise overpowered the groans of the victims; the enclosure was broken and overturned by the mob. Like madmen, they rushed at the burning pile,—armed with sabres, axes, and knives, and snatching the bodies dead or alive from the flames, tore them to pieces, carrying off the bones to make whistles or handles for their daggers as a souvenir of this horrible day.

CHAPTER VI

The spectacle of this frightful punishment did not satisfy the revenge of Charles of Durazzo. Seconded by the chief-justice, he daily brought about fresh executions, till Andre's death came to be no more than a pretext for the legal murder of all who opposed his projects. But Louis of Tarentum, who had won Joan's heart, and was eagerly trying to get the necessary dispensation for legalising the marriage, from this time forward took as a personal insult every act of the high court of justice which was performed against his will and against the queen's prerogative: he armed all his adherents, increasing their number by all the adventurers he could get together, and so put on foot a strong enough force to support his own party and resist his cousin. Naples was thus split up into hostile camps, ready to come to blows on the smallest pretext, whose daily skirmishes, moreover, were always followed by some scene of pillage or death.

But Louis had need of money both to pay his mercenaries and to hold his own against the Duke of Durazzo and his own brother Robert, and one day he discovered that the queen's coffers were empty. Joan was wretched and desperate, and her lover, though generous and brave and anxious to reassure her so far as he could, did not very clearly see how to extricate himself from such a difficult situation. But his mother Catherine, whose ambition was satisfied in seeing one of her sons, no matter which, attain to the throne of Naples, came unexpectedly to their aid, promising solemnly that it would only take her a few days to be able to lay at her niece's feet a treasure richer than anything she had ever dreamed of, queen as she was.

The empress then took half her son's troops, made for Saint Agatha, and besieged the fortress where Charles and Bertrand of Artois had taken refuge when they fled from justice. The old count, astonished at the sight of this woman, who had been the very soul of the conspiracy, and not in the least understanding her arrival as an enemy, sent out to ask the intention of this display of military force. To which Catherine replied in words which we translate literally:

"My friends, tell Charles, our faithful friend, that we desire to speak with him privately and alone concerning a matter equally interesting to us both, and he is not to be alarmed at our arriving in the guise of an enemy, for this we have done designedly, as we shall explain in the course of our interview. We know he is confined to bed by the gout, and therefore feel no surprise at his not coming out to meet us. Have the goodness to salute him on our part and reassure him, telling him that we desire to come in, if such is his good pleasure, with our intimate counsellor, Nicholas Acciajuoli, and ten soldiers only, to speak with him concerning an important matter that cannot be entrusted to go-betweens."

Entirely reassured by these frank, friendly explanations, Charles of Artois sent out his son Bertrand to the empress to receive her with the respect due to her rank and high position at the court of Naples. Catherine went promptly to the castle with many signs of joy, and inquiring after the count's health and expressing her affection, as soon as they were alone, she mysteriously lowered her voice and explained that the object of her visit was to consult a man of tried experience on the affairs of Naples, and to beg his active cooperation in the queen's favour. As, however, she was not pressed for time, she could wait at Saint Agatha for the count's recovery to hear his views and tell him of the march of events since he left the court. She succeeded so well in gaining the old man's confidence and banishing his suspicions, that he begged her to honour them with her presence as long as she was able, and little by little received all her men within the walls. This was what Catherine was waiting for: on the very day when her army was installed at Saint Agatha, she suddenly entered the count's room, followed by four soldiers, and seizing the old man by the throat, exclaimed wrathfully—

"Miserable traitor, you will not escape from our hands before you have received the punishment you deserve. In the meanwhile, show me where your treasure is hidden, if you would not have me throw your body out to feed the crows that are swooping around these dungeons."

The count, half choking, the dagger at his breast, did not even attempt to call for help; he fell on his knees, begging the empress to save at least the life of his son, who was not yet well from the terrible attack of melancholia that had shaken his reason ever since the catastrophe. Then he painfully dragged himself to the place where he had hidden his treasure, and pointing with his finger, cried—

"Take all; take my life; but spare my son."

Catherine could not contain herself for joy when she saw spread out at her feet exquisite and incredibly valuable cups, caskets of pearls, diamonds and rubies of marvellous value, coffers full of gold ingots, and all the wonders of Asia that surpass the wildest imagination. But when the old man, trembling, begged for the liberty of his son as the price of his fortune and his own life, the empress resumed her cold, pitiless manner, and harshly replied—

"I have already given orders for your son to be brought here; but prepare for an eternal farewell, for he is to be taken to the fortress of Melfi, and you in all probability will end your days beneath the castle of Saint Agatha."

The grief of the poor count at this violent separation was so great, that a few days later he was found dead in his dungeon, his lips covered with a bloody froth, his hands gnawed in despair. Bertrand did not long survive him. He actually lost his reason when he heard of his father's death, and hanged himself on the prison grating. Thus did the murderers of Andre destroy one another, like venomous animals shut up in the same cage.

Catherine of Tarentum, carrying off the treasure she had so gained, arrived at the court of Naples, proud of her triumph and contemplating vast schemes. But new troubles had come about in her absence. Charles of Durazzo, for the last time desiring the queen to give him the duchy of Calabria, a title which had always belonged to the heir presumptive, and angered by her refusal, had written to Louis of Hungary, inviting him to take possession of the kingdom, and promising to help in the enterprise with all his own forces, and to give up the principal authors of his brother's death, who till now had escaped justice.

The King of Hungary eagerly accepted these offers, and got ready an army to avenge Andre's death and proceed to the conquest of Naples. The tears of his mother Elizabeth and the advice of Friar Robert, the old minister, who had fled to Buda, confirmed him in his projects of vengeance. He had already lodged a bitter complaint at the court of Avignon that, while the inferior assassins had been punished, she who was above all others guilty had been shamefully let off scot free, and though still stained with her husband's blood, continued to live a life of debauchery and adultery. The pope replied soothingly that, so far as it depended upon him, he would not be found slow to give satisfaction to a lawful grievance; but the accusation ought to be properly formulated and supported by proof; that no doubt Joan's conduct during and after her husband's death was blamable; but His Majesty must consider that the Church of Rome, which before all things seeks truth and justice, always proceeds with the utmost circumspection, and in so grave a matter more especially must not judge by appearances only.

Joan, frightened by the preparations for war, sent ambassadors to the Florentine Republic, to assert her innocence of the crime imputed to her by public opinion, and did not hesitate to send excuses even to the Hungarian court; but Andre's brother replied in a letter laconic and threatening:—

"Your former disorderly life, the arrogation to yourself of exclusive power, your neglect to punish your husband's murderers, your marriage to another husband, moreover your own excuses, are all sufficient proofs that you were an accomplice in the murder."

Catherine would not be put out of heart by the King of Hungary's threats, and looking at the position of the queen and her son with a coolness that was never deceived, she was convinced that there was no other means of safety except a reconciliation with Charles, their mortal foe, which could only be brought about by giving him all he wanted. It was one of two things: either he would help them to repulse the King of Hungary, and later on they would pay the cost when the dangers were less pressing, or he would be beaten himself, and thus they would at least have the pleasure of drawing him down with them in their own destruction.

The agreement was made in the gardens of Castel Nuovo, whither Charles had repaired on the invitation of the queen and her aunt. To her cousin of Durazzo Joan accorded the title so much desired of Duke of Calabria, and Charles, feeling that he was hereby made heir to the kingdom, marched at once on Aquila, which town already was flying the Hungarian colours. The wretched man did not foresee that he was going straight to his destruction.

When the Empress of Constantinople saw this man, whom she hated above all others, depart in joy, she looked contemptuously upon him, divining by a woman's instinct that mischief would befall him; then, having no further mischief to do, no further treachery on earth, no further revenge to satisfy, she all at once succumbed to some unknown malady, and died suddenly, without uttering a cry or exciting a single regret.

But the King of Hungary, who had crossed Italy with a formidable army, now entered the kingdom from the side of Aquila: on his way he had everywhere received marks of interest and sympathy; and Alberto and Mertino delta Scala, lords of Verona, had given him three hundred horse to prove that all their goodwill was with him in his enterprise. The news of the arrival of the Hungarians threw the court into a state of confusion impossible to describe. They had hoped that the king would be stopped by the pope's legate, who had come to Foligno to forbid him, in the name of the Holy Father, and on pain of excommunication to proceed any further without his consent; but Louis of Hungary replied to the pope's legate that, once master of Naples, he should consider himself a feudatory of the Church, but till then he had no obligations except to God and his own conscience. Thus the avenging army fell like a thunderbolt upon the heart of the kingdom, before there was any thought of taking serious measures for defence. There was only one plan possible: the queen assembled the barons who were most strongly attached to her, made them swear homage and fidelity to Louis of Tarentum, whom she presented to them as her husband, and then leaving with many tears her most faithful subjects, she embarked secretly, in the middle of the night, on a ship of Provence, and made for Marseilles. Louis of Tarentum, following the prompting of his adventure-loving character, left Naples at the head of three thousand horse and a considerable number of foot, and took up his post on the banks of the Voltorno, there to contest the enemy's passage; but the King of Hungary foresaw the stratagem, and while his adversary was waiting for him at Capua, he arrived at Beneventum by the mountains of Alife and Morcone, and on the same day received Neapolitan envoys: they in a magnificent display of eloquence congratulated him on his entrance, offered the keys of the town, and swore obedience to him as being the legitimate successor of Charles of Anjou. The news of the surrender of Naples soon reached the queen's camp, and all the princes of the blood and the generals left Louis of Tarentum and took refuge in the capital. Resistance was impossible. Louis, accompanied by his counsellor, Nicholas Acciajuoli, went to Naples on the same evening on which his relatives quitted the town to get away from the enemy. Every hope of safety was vanishing as the hours passed by; his brothers and cousins begged him to go at once, so as not to draw down upon the town the king's vengeance, but unluckily there was no ship in the harbour that was ready to set sail. The terror of the princes was at its height; but Louis, trusting in his luck, started with the brave Acciajuoli in an unseaworthy boat, and ordering four sailors to row with all their might, in a few minutes disappeared, leaving his family in a great state of anxiety till they learned that he had reached Pisa, whither he had gone to join the queen in Provence. Charles of Durazzo and Robert of Tarentum, who were the eldest respectively of the two branches of the royal family, after hastily consulting, decided to soften the Hungarian monarch's wrath by a complete submission. Leaving their young brothers at Naples, they accordingly set off for Aversa, where the king was. Louis received them with every mark of friendship, and asked with much interest why their brothers were not with them. The princes replied that their young brothers had stayed at Naples to prepare a worthy reception for His Majesty. Louis thanked them for their kind intentions, but begged them to invite the young princes now, saying that it would be infinitely more pleasant to enter Naples with all his family, and that he was most anxious to see his cousins. Charles and Robert, to please the king, sent equerries to bid their brothers come to Aversa; but Louis of Durazzo, the eldest of the boys, with many tears begged the others not to obey, and sent a message that he was prevented by a violent headache from leaving Naples. So puerile an excuse could not fail to annoy Charles, and the same day he compelled the unfortunate boys to appear before the king, sending a formal order which admitted of no delay. Louis of Hungary embraced them warmly one after the other, asked them several questions in an affectionate way, kept them to supper, and only let them go quite late at night.

When the Duke of Durazzo reached his room, Lello of Aquila and the Count of Fondi slipped mysteriously to the side of his bed, and making sure that no one could hear, told him that the king in a council held that morning had decided to kill him and to imprison the other princes. Charles heard them out, but incredulously: suspecting treachery, he dryly replied that he had too much confidence in his cousin's loyalty to believe such a black calumny. Lello insisted, begging him in the name of his dearest friends to listen; but the duke was impatient, and harshly ordered him to depart.

The next day there was the same kindness on the king's part, the same affection shown to the children, the same invitation to supper. The banquet was magnificent; the room was brilliantly lighted, and the reflections were dazzling: vessels of gold shone on the table; the intoxicating perfume of flowers filled the air; wine foamed in the goblets and flowed from the flagons in ruby streams; conversation, excited and discursive, was heard on every side; all faces beamed with joy.

Charles of Durazzo sat opposite the king, at a separate table among his brothers. Little by little his look grew fixed, his brow pensive. He was fancying that Andre might have supped in this very hall on the eve of his tragic end, and he thought how all concerned in that death had either died in torment or were now languishing in prison; the queen, an exile and a fugitive, was begging pity from strangers: he alone was free. The thought made him tremble; but admiring his own cleverness in pursuing his infernal schemes, and putting away his sad looks, he smiled again with an expression of indefinable pride. The madman at this moment was scoffing at the justice of God. But Lello of Aquila, who was waiting at the table, bent down, whispering gloomily

"Unhappy duke, why did you refuse to believe me? Fly, while there is yet time."

Charles, angered by the man's obstinacy, threatened that if he were such a fool as to say any more, he would repeat every word aloud.

"I have done my duty," murmured Lello, bowing his head; "now it must happen as God wills."

As he left off speaking, the king rose, and as the duke went up to take his leave, his face suddenly changed, and he cried in an awful voice—

"Traitor! At length you are in my hands, and you shall die as you deserve; but before you are handed over to the executioner, confess with your own lips your deeds of treachery towards our royal majesty: so shall we need no other witness to condemn you to a punishment proportioned to your crimes. Between our two selves, Duke of Durazzo, tell me first why, by your infamous manoeuvring, you aided your uncle, the Cardinal of Perigord, to hinder the coronation of my brother, and so led him on, since he had no royal prerogative of his own, to his miserable end? Oh, make no attempt to deny it. Here is the letter sealed with your seal; in secret you wrote it, but it accuses you in public. Then why, after bringing us hither to avenge our brother's death, of which you beyond all doubt were the cause,—why did you suddenly turn to the queen's party and march against our town of Aquila, daring to raise an army against our faithful subjects? You hoped, traitor, to make use of us as a footstool to mount the throne withal, as soon as you were free from every other rival. Then you would but have awaited our departure to kill the viceroy we should have left in our place, and so seize the kingdom.

But this time your foresight has been at fault. There is yet another crime worse than all the rest, a crime of high treason, which I shall remorselessly punish. You carried off the bride that our ancestor King Robert designed for me, as you knew, by his will. Answer, wretch what excuse can you make for the rape of the Princess Marie?"

Anger had so changed Louis's voice that the last words sounded like the roar of a wild beast: his eyes glittered with a feverish light, his lips were pale and trembling. Charles and his brothers fell upon their knees, frozen by mortal terror, and the unhappy duke twice tried to speak, but his teeth were chattering so violently that he could not articulate a single word. At last, casting his eyes about him and seeing his poor brothers, innocent and ruined by his fault, he regained some sort of courage, and said—

"My lord, you look upon me with a terrible countenance that makes me tremble. But on my knees I entreat you, have mercy on me if I have done wrong, for God is my witness that I did not call you to this kingdom with any criminal intention: I have always desired, and still desire, your supremacy in all the sincerity of my soul. Some treacherous counsellors, I am certain, have contrived to draw down your hatred upon me. If it is true, as you say, that I went with an armed force to Aquila I was compelled by Queen Joan, and I could not do otherwise; but as soon as I heard of your arrival at Fermo I took my troops away again. I hope for the love of Christ I may obtain your mercy and pardon, by reason of my former services and constant loyalty. But as I see you are now angry with me, I say no more waiting for your fury to pass over. Once again, my lord, have pity upon us, since we are in the hands of your Majesty."

The king turned away his head, and retired slowly, confiding the prisoners to the care of Stephen Vayvoda and the Count of Zornic, who guarded them during the night in a room adjoining the king's chamber. The next day Louis held another meeting of his council, and ordered that Charles should have his throat cut on the very spot where poor Andre had been hanged. He then sent the other princes of the blood, loaded with chains, to Hungary, where they were long kept prisoners. Charles, quite thunderstruck by such an unexpected blow, overwhelmed by the thought of his past crimes, trembled like a coward face to face with death, and seemed completely crushed. Bowed, upon his knees, his face half hidden in his hands, from time to time convulsive sobs escaped him, as he tried to fix the thoughts that chased each other through his mind like the shapes of a monstrous dream. Night was in his soul, but every now and then light flashed across the darkness, and over the gloomy background of his despair passed gilded figures fleeing from him with smiles of mockery. In his ears buzzed voices from the other world; he saw a long procession of ghosts, like the conspirators whom Nicholas of Melazzo had pointed out in the vaults of Castel Nuovo. But these phantoms each held his head in his hand, and shaking it by the hair, bespattered him with drops of blood. Some brandished whips, some knives: each threatened Charles with his instrument of torture. Pursued by the nocturnal train, the hapless man opened his mouth for one mighty cry, but his breath was gone, and it died upon his lips. Then he beheld his mother stretching out her arms from afar, and he fancied that if he could but reach her he would be safe. But at each step the path grew more and more narrow, pieces of his flesh were torn off by the approaching walls; at last, breathless, naked and bleeding, he reached his goal; but his mother glided farther away, and it was all to begin over again. The phantoms pursued him, grinning and screaming in his ears:—

"Cursed be he who slayeth his mother!"

Charles was roused from these horrors by the cries of his brothers, who had come to embrace him for the last time before embarking. The duke in a low voice asked their pardon, and then fell back into his state of despair. The children were dragged away, begging to be allowed to share their brother's fate, and crying for death as an alleviation of their woes. At length they were separated, but the sound of their lamentation sounded long in the heart of the condemned man. After a few moments, two soldiers and two equerries came to tell the duke that his hour had come.

Charles followed them, unresisting, to the fatal balcony where Andre had been hanged. He was there asked if he desired to confess, and when he said yes, they brought a monk from the sane convent where the terrible scene had been enacted: he listened to the confession of all his sins, and granted him absolution. The duke at once rose and walked to the place where Andre had been thrown down for the cord to be put round his neck, and there, kneeling again, he asked his executioners—

"Friends, in pity tell me, is there any hope for my life?"

And when they answered no, Charles exclaimed:

"Then carry out your instructions."

At these words, one of the equerries plunged his sword into his breast, and the other cut his head off with a knife, and his corpse was thrown over the balcony into the garden where Andre's body had lain for three days unburied.

CHAPTER VII

The King of Hungary, his black flag ever borne before him, started for Naples, refusing all offered honours, and rejecting the canopy beneath which he was to make his entry, not even stopping to give audience to the chief citizens or to receive the acclamations of the crowd. Armed at all points, he made for Castel Nuovo, leaving behind him dismay and fear. His first act on entering the city was to order Dona Cancha to be burnt, her punishment having been deferred by reason of her pregnancy. Like the others, she was drawn on a cart to the square of St. Eligius, and there consigned to the flames. The young creature, whose suffering had not impaired her beauty, was dressed as for a festival, and laughing like a mad thing up to the last moment, mocked at her executioners and threw kisses to the crowd.

A few days later, Godfrey of Marsana, Count of Squillace and grand admiral of the kingdom, was arrested by the king's orders. His life was promised him on condition of his delivering up Conrad of Catanzaro, one of his relatives, accused of conspiring against Andre. The grand admiral committed this act of shameless treachery, and did not shrink from sending his own son to persuade Conrad to come to the town. The poor wretch was given over to the king, and tortured alive on a wheel made with sharp knives. The sight of these barbarities, far from calming the king's rage, seemed to inflame it the more. Every day there were new accusations and new sentences. The prisons were crowded: Louis's punishments were redoubled in severity. A fear arose that the town, and indeed the whole kingdom, were to be treated as having taken part in Andre's death. Murmurs arose against this barbarous rule, and all men's thoughts turned towards their fugitive queen. The Neapolitan barons had taken the oath of fidelity with no willing hearts; and when it came to the turn of the Counts of San Severino, they feared a trick of some kind, and refused to appear all together before the Hungarian, but took refuge in the town of Salerno, and sent Archbishop Roger, their brother, to make sure of the king's intentions beforehand. Louis received him magnificently, and appointed him privy councillor and grand proto notary. Then, and not till then, did Robert of San Severino and Roger, Count of Chiaramonte, venture into the king's presence; after doing homage, they retired to their homes. The other barons followed their example of caution, and hiding their discontent under a show of respect, awaited a favourable moment for shaking off the foreign yoke. But the queen had encountered no obstacle in her flight, and arrived at Nice five days later. Her passage through Provence was like a triumph. Her beauty, youth, and misfortunes, even certain mysterious reports as to her adventures, all contributed to arouse the interest of the Provencal people. Games and fetes were improvised to soften the hardship of exile for the proscribed princess; but amid the outbursts of joy from every town, castle, and city, Joan, always sad, lived ever in her silent grief and glowing memories.

At the gates of Aix she found the clergy, the nobility,

and the chief magistrates, who received her respectfully but with no signs of enthusiasm. As the queen advanced, her astonishment increased as she saw the coldness of the people and the solemn, constrained air of the great men who escorted her. Many anxious thoughts alarmed her, and she even went so far as to fear some intrigue of the King of Hungary. Scarcely had her cortege arrived at Castle Arnaud, when the nobles, dividing into two ranks, let the queen pass with her counsellor Spinelli and two women; then closing up, they cut her off from the rest of her suite. After this, each in turn took up his station as guardian of the fortress.

There was no room for doubt: the queen was a prisoner; but the cause of the manoeuvre it was impossible to guess. She asked the high dignitaries, and they, protesting respectful devotion, refused to explain till they had news from Avignon. Meanwhile all honours that a queen could receive were lavished on Joan; but she was kept in sight and forbidden to go out. This new trouble increased her depression: she did not know what had happened to Louis of Tarentum, and her imagination, always apt at creating disasters, instantly suggested that she would soon be weeping for his loss.

But Louis, always with his faithful Acciajuoli, had after many fatiguing adventures been shipwrecked at the port of Pisa; thence he had taken route for Florence, to beg men and money; but the Florentines decided to keep an absolute neutrality, and refused to receive him. The prince, losing his last hope, was pondering gloomy plans, when Nicholas Acciajuoli thus resolutely addressed him:

"My lord, it is not given to mankind to enjoy prosperity for ever: there are misfortunes beyond all human foresight. You were once rich and powerful, and you are now a fugitive in disguise, begging the help of others. You must reserve your strength for better days. I still have a considerable fortune, and also have relations and friends whose wealth is at my disposal: let us try to make our way to the queen, and at once decide what we can do. I myself shall always defend you and obey you as my lord and master."

The prince received these generous offers with the utmost gratitude, and told his counsellor that he placed his person in his hands and all that remained of his future. Acciajuoli, not content with serving his master as a devoted servant, persuaded his brother Angelo, Archbishop of Florence, who was in great favour at Clement VI's court, to join with them in persuading the pope to interest himself in the cause of Louis of Tarentum. So, without further delay, the prince, his counsellor, and the good prelate made their way to the port of Marseilles, but learning that the queen was a prisoner at Aix, they embarked at Acque-Morte, and went straight to Avignon. It soon appeared that the pope had a real affection and esteem for the character of the Archbishop of Florence, for Louis was received with paternal kindness at the court of Avignon; which was far more than he had expected: when he kneeled before the sovereign pontiff, His Holiness bent affectionately towards him and helped him to rise, saluting him by the title of king.

Two days later, another prelate, the Archbishop of Aix,

came into the queen's presence,—

"Most gracious and dearly beloved sovereign, permit the most humble and devoted of your servants to ask pardon, in the name of your subjects, for the painful but necessary measure they have thought fit to take concerning your Majesty. When you arrived on our coast, your loyal town of Aix had learned from a trustworthy source that the King of France was proposing to give our country to one of his own sons, making good this loss to you by the cession of another domain, also that the Duke of Normandy had come to Avignon to request this exchange in person. We were quite decided, madam, and had made a vow to God that we would give up everything rather than suffer the hateful tyranny of the French. But before spilling blood we thought it best to secure your august person as a sacred hostage, a sacred ark which no man dared touch but was smitten to the ground, which indeed must keep away from our walls the scourge of war. We have now read the formal annulment of this hateful plan, in a brief sent by the sovereign pontiff from Avignon; and in this brief he himself guarantees your good faith.

"We give you your full and entire liberty, and henceforth we shall only endeavour to keep you among us by prayers and protestations. Go then, madam, if that is your pleasure, but before you leave these lands, which will be plunged into mourning by your withdrawal, leave with us some hope that you forgive the apparent violence to which we have subjected you, only in the fear that we might lose you; and remember that on the day when you cease to be our queen you sign the death-warrant of all your subjects."

Joan reassured the archbishop and the deputation from her good town of Aix with a melancholy smile, and promised that she would always cherish the memory of their affection. For this time she could not be deceived as to the real sentiments of the nobles and people; and a fidelity so uncommon, revealed with sincere tears, touched her heart and made her reflect bitterly upon her past. But a league's distance from Avignon a magnificent triumphal reception awaited her. Louis of Tarentum and all the cardinals present at the court had come out to meet her. Pages in dazzling dress carried above Joan's head a canopy of scarlet velvet, ornamented with fleur-de-lys in gold and plumes. Handsome youths and lovely girls, their heads crowned with flowers, went before her singing her praise. The streets were bordered with a living hedge of people; the houses were decked out; the bells rang a triple peal, as at the great Church festivals. Clement VI first received the queen at the castle of Avignon with all the pomp he knew so well how to employ on solemn occasions, then she was lodged in the palace of Cardinal Napoleon of the Orsini, who on his return from the Conclave at Perugia had built this regal dwelling at Villeneuve, inhabited later by the popes.

No words could give an idea of the strangely disturbed condition of Avignon at this period. Since Clement V had transported the seat of the papacy to Provence, there had sprung up, in this rival to Rome, squares, churches, cardinals' palaces, of unparalleled splendour. All the business of nations and kings was transacted at the castle of Avignon. Ambassadors from every court, merchants of every nation, adventurers of all kinds, Italians, Spaniards, Hungarians, Arabs, Jews, soldiers, Bohemians, jesters, poets, monks, courtesans, swarmed and clustered here, and hustled one another in the streets. There was confusion of tongues, customs, and costumes, an inextricable mixture of splendour and rags, riches and misery, debasement and grandeur. The austere poets of the Middle Ages stigmatised the accursed city in their writings under the name of the New Babylon.

There is one curious monument of Joan's sojourn at Avignon and the exercise of her authority as sovereign. She was indignant at the effrontery of the women of the town, who elbowed everybody shamelessly in the streets, and published a notable edict, the first of its kind, which has since served as a model in like cases, to compel all unfortunate women who trafficked in their honour to live shut up together in a house, that was bound to be open every day in the year except the last three days of Holy Week, the entrance to be barred to Jews at all times. An abbess, chosen once a year, had the supreme control over this strange convent. Rules were established for the maintenance of order, and severe penalties inflicted for any infringement of discipline. The lawyers of the period gained a great reputation by this salutary institution; the fair ladies of Avignon were eager in their defence of the queen in spite of the calumnious reports that strove to tarnish her reputation: with one voice the wisdom of Andre's widow was extolled. The concert of praises was disturbed, however, by murmurs from the recluses themselves, who, in their own brutal language, declared that Joan of Naples was impeding their commerce so as to get a monopoly for herself.

Meanwhile Marie of Durazzo had joined her sister. After her husband's death she had found means to take refuge in the convent of Santa Croce with her two little daughters; and while Louis of Hungary was busy burning his victims, the unhappy Marie had contrived to make her escape in the frock of an old monk, and as by a miracle to get on board a ship that was setting sail for Provence. She related to her sister the frightful details of the king's cruelty. And soon a new proof of his implacable hatred confirmed the tales of the poor princess.

Louis's ambassadors appeared at the court of Avignon to demand formally the queen's condemnation.

It was a great day when Joan of Naples pleaded her own cause before the pope, in the presence of all the cardinals then at Avignon, all the ambassadors of foreign powers, and all the eminent persons come from every quarter of Europe to be present at this trial, unique in the annals of history. We must imagine a vast enclosure, in whose midst upon a raised throne, as president of the august tribunal, sat God's vicar on earth, absolute and supreme judge, emblem of temporal and spiritual power, of authority human and divine. To right and left of the sovereign pontiff, the cardinals in their red robes sat in chairs set round in a circle, and behind these princes of the Sacred College stretched rows of bishops extending to the end of the hall, with vicars, canons, deacons, archdeacons, and the whole immense hierarchy of the Church. Facing the pontifical throne was a platform reserved for the Queen of Naples and her suite. At the pope's feet stood the ambassadors from the King of Hungary, who played the part of accusers without speaking a word, the circumstances of the crime and all the proofs having been discussed beforehand by a committee appointed for the purpose. The rest of the hall was filled by a brilliant crowd of high dignitaries, illustrious captains, and noble envoys, all vying with one another in proud display. Everyone ceased to breathe, all eyes were fixed on the dais whence Joan was to speak her own defence. A movement of uneasy curiosity made this compact mass of humanity surge towards the centre, the cardinals above raised like proud peacocks over a golden harvest-field shaken in the breeze.

The queen appeared, hand in hand with her uncle, the old Cardinal of Perigord, and her aunt, the Countess Agnes. Her gait was so modest and proud, her countenance so melancholy and pure, her looks so open and confident, that even before she spoke every heart was hers. Joan was now twenty years of age; her magnificent beauty was fully developed, but an extreme pallor concealed the brilliance of her transparent satin skin, and her hollow cheek told the tale of expiation and suffering. Among the spectators who looked on most eagerly there was a certain young man with strongly marked features, glowing eyes, and brown hair, whom we shall meet again later on in our narrative; but we will not divert our readers' attention, but only tell them that his name was James of Aragon, that he was Prince of Majorca, and would have been ready to shed every drop of his blood only to check one single tear that hung on Joan's eyelids. The queen spoke in an agitated, trembling voice, stopping from time to time to dry her moist and shining eyes, or to breathe one of those deep sighs that go straight to the heart. She told the tale of her husband's death painfully and vividly, painted truthfully the mad terror that had seized upon her and struck her down at that frightful time, raised her hands to her brow with the gesture of despair, as though she would wrest the madness from her brain—and a shudder of pity and awe passed through the assembled crowd. It is a fact that at this moment, if her words were false, her anguish was both sincere and terrible. An angel soiled by crime, she lied like Satan himself, but like him too she suffered all the agony of remorse and pride. Thus, when at the end of her speech she burst into tears and implored help and protection against the usurper of her kingdom, a cry of general assent drowned her closing words, several hands flew to their sword-hilts, and the Hungarian ambassadors retired covered with shame and confusion.

That same evening the sentence, to the great joy of all, was proclaimed, that Joan was innocent and acquitted of all concern in the assassination of her husband. But as her conduct after the event and the indifference she had shown about pursuing the authors of the crime admitted of no valid excuse, the pope declared that there were plain traces of magic, and that the wrong-doing attributed to Joan was the result of some baneful charm cast upon her, which she could by no possible means resist. At the same time, His Holiness confirmed her marriage with Louis of Tarentum, and bestowed on him the order of the Rose of Gold and the title of King of Sicily and Jerusalem. Joan, it is true, had on the eve of her acquittal sold the town of Avignon to the pope for the sum of 80,000 florins.

While the queen was pleading her cause at the court of Clement VI, a dreadful epidemic, called the Black Plague—the same that Boccaccio has described so wonderfully—was ravaging the kingdom of Naples, and indeed the whole of Italy. According to the calculation of Matteo Villani, Florence lost three-fifths of her population, Bologna two-thirds, and nearly all Europe was reduced in some such frightful proportion. The Neapolitans were already weary of the cruelties and greed of the Hungarians, they were only awaiting some opportunity to revolt against the stranger's oppression, and to recall their lawful sovereign, whom, for all her ill deeds, they had never ceased to love. The attraction of youth and beauty was deeply felt by this pleasure-loving people. Scarcely had the pestilence thrown confusion into the army and town, when loud cursing arose against the tyrant and his executioners. Louis of Hungary, suddenly threatened by the wrath of Heaven and the people's vengeance, was terrified both by the plague and by the riots, and disappeared in the middle of the night. Leaving the government of Naples in the hands of Conrad Lupo, one of his captains, he embarked hastily at Berletta, and left the kingdom in very much the same way as Louis of Tarentum, fleeing from him, had left it a few months before.

This news arrived at Avignon just when the pope was about to send the queen his bull of absolution. It was at once decided to take away the kingdom from Louis's viceroy. Nicholas Acciajuoli left for Naples with the marvellous bull that was to prove to all men the innocence of the queen, to banish all scruples and stir up a new enthusiasm. The counsellor first went to the castle of Melzi, commanded by his son Lorenzo: this was the only fortress that had always held out. The father and son embraced with the honourable pride that near relatives may justly feel when they meet after they have united in the performance of a heroic duty. From the governor of Melzi Louis of Tarentum's counsellor learned that all men were wearied of the arrogance and vexatious conduct of the queen's enemies, and that a conspiracy was in train, started in the University of Naples, but with vast ramifications all over the kingdom, and moreover that there was dissension in the enemy's army. The indefatigable counsellor went from Apulia to Naples, traversing towns and villages, collecting men everywhere, proclaiming loudly the acquittal of the queen and her marriage with Louis of Tarentum, also that the pope was offering indulgences to such as would receive with joy their lawful sovereigns. Then seeing that the people shouted as he went by, "Long live Joan! Death to the Hungarians!" he returned and told his sovereigns in what frame of mind he had left their subjects.

Joan borrowed money wherever she could, armed galleys,

and left Marseilles with her husband, her sister, and two faithful advisers, Acciajuoli and Spinelli, on the 10th of September 1348. The king and queen not being able to enter at the harbour, which was in the enemy's power, disembarked at Santa Maria del Carmine, near the river Sebeto, amid the frenzied applause of an immense crowd, and accompanied by all the Neapolitan nobles. They made their way to the palace of Messire Ajutorio, near Porta Capuana, the Hungarians having fortified themselves in all the castles; but Acciajuoli, at the head of the queen's partisans, blockaded the fortresses so ably that half of the enemy were obliged to surrender, and the other half took to flight and were scattered about the interior of the kingdom. We shall now follow Louis of Tarentum in his arduous adventures in Apulia, the Calabrias, and the Abruzzi, where he recovered one by one the fortresses that the Hungarians had taken. By dint of unexampled valour and patience, he at last mastered nearly all the more considerable places, when suddenly everything changed, and fortune turned her back upon him for the second time. A German captain called Warner, who had deserted the Hungarian army to sell himself to the queen, had again played the traitor and sold himself once more, allowed himself to be surprised at Corneto by Conrad Lupo, the King of Hungary's vicar-general, and openly joined him, taking along with him a great party of the adventurers who fought under his orders. This unexpected defection forced Louis of Tarentum to retire to Naples. The King of Hungary soon learning that the troops had rallied round his banner, and only awaited his return to march upon the capital, disembarked with a strong reinforcement of cavalry at the port of Manfredonia, and taking Trani, Canosa, and Salerno, went forward to lay siege to Aversa.

The news fell like a thunder-clap on Joan and her husband. The Hungarian army consisted of 10,000 horse and more than 7000 infantry, and Aversa had only 500 soldiers under Giacomo Pignatelli. In spite of the immense disproportion of the numbers, the Neapolitan general vigorously repelled the attack; and the King of Hungary, fighting in the front, was wounded in his foot by an arrow. Then Louis, seeing that it would be difficult to take the place by storm, determined to starve them out. For three months the besieged performed prodigies of valour, and further assistance was impossible. Their capitulation was expected at any moment, unless indeed they decided to perish every man. Renaud des Baux, who was to come from Marseilles with a squadron of ten ships to defend the ports of the capital and secure the queen's flight, should the Hungarian army get possession of Naples, had been delayed by adverse winds and obliged to stop on the way. All things seemed to conspire in favour of the enemy. Louis of Tarentum, whose generous soul refused to shed the blood of his brave men in an unequal and desperate struggle, nobly sacrificed himself, and made an offer to the King of Hungary to settle their quarrel in single combat. We append the authentic letters that passed between Joan's husband and Andre's brother.

"Illustrious King of Hungary, who has come to invade

our kingdom, we, by the grace of God King of Jerusalem and Sicily, invite you to single combat. We know that you are in no wise disturbed by the death of your lancers or the other pagans in your suite, no more indeed than if they were dogs; but we, fearing harm to our own soldiers and men-at-arms, desire to fight with you personally, to put an end to the present war and restore peace to our kingdom. He who survives shall be king. And therefore, to ensure that this duel shall take place, we definitely propose as a site either Paris, in the presence of the King of France, or one of the towns of Perugia, Avignon, or Naples. Choose one of these four places, and send us your reply."

The King of Hungary first consulted with his council, and then replied:—

"Great King, we have read and considered your letter sent to us by the bearer of these presents, and by your invitation to a duel we are most supremely pleased; but we do not approve of any of the places you propose, since they are all suspect, and for several reasons. The King of France is your maternal grandfather, and although we are also connected by blood with him, the relationship is not so near. The town of Avignon, although nominally belonging to the sovereign pontiff, is the capital of Provence, and has always been subject to your rule. Neither have we any more confidence in Perugia, for that town is devoted to your cause.

"As to the city of Naples, there is no need to say that we refuse that rendezvous, since it is in revolt against us and you are there as king. But if you wish to fight with us, let it be in the presence of the Emperor of Germany, who is lord supreme, or the King of England, who is our common friend, or the Patriarch of Aquilea, a good Catholic. If you do not approve of any of the places we propose, we shall soon be near you with our army, and so remove all difficulties and delays. Then you can come forth, and our duel can take place in the presence of both armies."

After the interchange of these two letters, Louis of Tarentum proposed nothing further. The garrison at Aversa had capitulated after a heroic resistance, and it was known only too well that if the King of Hungary could get so far as the walls of Naples, he would not have to endanger his life in order to seize that city. Happily the Provencal galleys had reached port at last. The king and the queen had only just time to embark and take refuge at Gaeta. The Hungarian army arrived at Naples. The town was on the point of yielding, and had sent messengers to the king humbly demanding peace; but the speeches of the Hungarians showed such insolence that the people, irritated past endurance, took up arms, and resolved to defend their household gods with all the energy of despair.

CHAPTER VIII

While the Neapolitans were holding out against their enemy at the Porta Capuana, a strange scene was being enacted at the other side of the town, a scene that shows us in lively colours the violence and treachery of this barbarous age. The widow of Charles of Durazzo was shut up in the castle of Ovo, and awaiting in feverish anxiety the arrival of the ship that was to take her to the queen. The poor Princess Marie, pressing her weeping children to her heart, pale, with dishevelled locks, fixed eyes, and drawn lips, was listening for every sound, distracted between hope and fear. Suddenly steps resounded along the corridor; a friendly voice was heard; Marie fell upon her knees with a cry of joy: her liberator had come.

Renaud des Baux, admiral of the Provencal squadron, respectfully advanced, followed by his eldest son Robert and his chaplain.

"God, I thank Thee!" exclaimed Marie, rising to her feet; "we are saved."

"One moment, madam," said Renaud, stopping her: "you are indeed saved, but upon one condition."

"A condition?" murmured the princess in surprise.

"Listen, madam. The King of Hungary, the avenger of Andre's murderers, the slayer of your husband, is at the gates of Naples; the people and soldiers will succumb, as soon as their last gallant effort is spent—the army of the conqueror is about to spread desolation and death throughout the city by fire and the sword. This time the Hungarian butcher will spare no victims: he will kill the mother before her children's eyes, the children in their mother's arms. The drawbridge of this castle is up and there are none on guard; every man who can wield a sword is now at the other end of the town. Woe to you, Marie of Durazzo, if the King of Hungary shall remember that you preferred his rival to him!"

"But have you not come here to save me?" cried Marie in a voice of anguish. "Joan, my sister, did she not command you to take me to her?"

"Your sister is no longer in the position to give orders," replied Renaud, with a disdainful smile. "She had nothing for me but thanks because I saved her life, and her husband's too, when he fled like a coward before the man whom he had dared to challenge to a duel."

Marie looked fixedly at the admiral to assure herself that it was really he who thus arrogantly talked about his masters. But she was terrified at his imperturbable expression, and said gently—

"As I owe my life and my children's lives solely to your generosity, I am grateful to you beyond all measure. But we must hurry, my lord: every moment I fancy I hear cries of vengeance, and you would not leave me now a prey to my brutal enemy?"

"God forbid, madam; I will save you at the risk of my life; but I have said already, I impose a condition."

"What is it?" said Marie, with forced calm.

"That you marry my son on the instant, in the presence of

our reverend chaplain."

"Rash man!" cried Marie, recoiling, her face scarlet with indignation and shame; "you dare to speak thus to the sister of your legitimate sovereign? Give thanks to God that I will pardon an insult offered, as I know, in a moment of madness; try by your devotion to make me forget what you have said."

The count, without one word, signed to his son and a priest to follow, and prepared to depart. As he crossed the threshold Marie ran to him, and clasping her hands, prayed him in God's name never to forsake her. Renaud stopped.

"I might easily take my revenge," he said, "for your affront when you refuse my son in your pride; but that business I leave to Louis of Hungary, who will acquit himself, no doubt, with credit."

"Have mercy on my poor daughters!" cried the princess; "mercy at least for my poor babes, if my own tears cannot move you."

"If you loved your children," said the admiral, frowning, "you would have done your duty at once."

"But I do not love your son!" cried Marie, proud but trembling. "O God, must a wretched woman's heart be thus trampled? You, father, a minister of truth and justice, tell this man that God must not be called on to witness an oath dragged from the weak and helpless!"

She turned to the admiral's son; and added, sobbing—

"You are young, perhaps you have loved: one day no doubt you will love. I appeal to your loyalty as a young man, to your courtesy as a knight, to all your noblest impulses;

join me, and turn your father away from his fatal project. You have never seen me before: you do not know but that in my secret heart I love another. Your pride should be revolted at the sight of an unhappy woman casting herself at your feet and imploring your favour and protection. One word from you, Robert, and I shall bless you every moment of my life: the memory of you will be graven in my heart like the memory of a guardian angel, and my children shall name you nightly in their prayers, asking God to grant your wishes. Oh, say, will you not save me? Who knows, later on I may love you—with real love."

"I must obey my father," Robert replied, never lifting his eyes to the lovely suppliant.

The priest was silent. Two minutes passed, and these four persons, each absorbed in his own thoughts, stood motionless as statues carved at the four corners of a tomb. Marie was thrice tempted to throw herself into the sea. But a confused distant sound suddenly struck upon her ears: little by little it drew nearer, voices were more distinctly heard; women in the street were uttering cries of distress—

"Fly, fly! God has forsaken us; the Hungarians are in the town!"

The tears of Marie's children were the answer to these cries; and little Margaret, raising her hands to her mother, expressed her fear in speech that was far beyond her years. Renaud, without one look at this touching picture, drew his son towards the door.

"Stay," said the princess, extending her hand with a

solemn gesture: "as God sends no other aid to my children, it is His will that the sacrifice be accomplished."

She fell on her knees before the priest, bending her head like a victim who offers her neck to the executioner. Robert des Baux took his place beside her, and the priest pronounced the formula that united them for ever, consecrating the infamous deed by a sacrilegious blessing.

"All is over!" murmured Marie of Durazzo, looking tearfully on her little daughters.

"No, all is not yet over," said the admiral harshly, pushing her towards another room; "before we leave, the marriage must be consummated."

"O just God!" cried the princess, in a voice torn with anguish, and she fell swooning to the floor.

Renaud des Baux directed his ships towards Marseilles, where he hoped to get his son crowned Count of Provence, thanks to his strange marriage with Marie of Durazzo. But this cowardly act of treason was not to go unpunished. The wind rose with fury, and drove him towards Gaeta, where the queen and her husband had just arrived. Renaud bade his sailors keep in the open, threatening to throw any man into the sea who dared to disobey him. The crew at first murmured; soon cries of mutiny rose on every side. The admiral, seeing he was lost, passed from threats to prayers. But the princess, who had recovered her senses at the first thunder-clap, dragged herself up to the bridge and screamed for help,

"Come to me, Louis! Come, my barons! Death to the

cowardly wretches who have outraged my honour!"

Louis of Tarentum jumped into a boat, followed by some ten of his bravest men, and, rowing rapidly, reached the ship. Then Marie told him her story in a word, and he turned upon the admiral a lightning glance, as though defying him to make any defence.

"Wretch!" cried the king, transfixing the traitor with his sword.

Then he had the son loaded with chains, and also the unworthy priest who had served as accomplice to the admiral, who now expiated his odious crime by death. He took the princess and her children in his boat, and re-entered the harbour.

The Hungarians, however, forcing one of the gates of Naples, marched triumphant to Castel Nuovo. But as they were crossing the Piazza delle Correggie, the Neapolitans perceived that the horses were so weak and the men so reduced by all they had undergone during the siege of Aversa that a mere puff of wind would dispense this phantom-like army. Changing from a state of panic to real daring, the people rushed upon their conquerors, and drove them outside the walls by which they had just entered. The sudden violent reaction broke the pride of the King of Hungary, and made him more tractable when Clement VI decided that he ought at last to interfere. A truce was concluded first from the month of February 1350 to the beginning of April 1351, and the next year this was converted into a real peace, Joan paying to the King of Hungary the sum of 300,000 florins for the expenses of the war.

After the Hungarians had gone, the pope sent a legate to crown Joan and Louis of Tarentum, and the 25th of May, the day of Pentecost, was chosen for the ceremony. All contemporary historians speak enthusiastically of this magnificent fete. Its details have been immortalised by Giotto in the frescoes of the church which from this day bore the name of L'Incoronata. A general amnesty was declared for all who had taken part in the late wars on either side, and the king and queen were greeted with shouts of joy as they solemnly paraded beneath the canopy, with all the barons of the kingdom in their train.

But the day's joy was impaired by an accident which to a superstitious people seemed of evil augury. Louis of Tarentum, riding a richly caparisoned horse, had just passed the Porta Petruccia, when some ladies looking out from a high window threw such a quantity of flowers at the king that his frightened steed reared and broke his rein. Louis could not hold him, so jumped lightly to the ground; but the crown fell at his feet and was broken into three pieces. On that very day the only daughter of Joan and Louis died.

But the king not wishing to sadden the brilliant ceremony with show of mourning, kept up the jousts and tournaments for three days, and in memory of his coronation instituted the order of 'Chevaliers du Noeud'. But from that day begun with an omen so sad, his life was nothing but a series of disillusions. After sustaining wars in Sicily and Apulia, and quelling the insurrection of Louis of Durazzo, who ended his days in the castle of Ovo, Louis of Tarentum, worn out by a life of pleasure, his health undermined by slow disease, overwhelmed with domestic trouble, succumbed to an acute fever on the 5th of June 1362, at the age of forty-two. His body had not been laid in its royal tomb at Saint Domenico before several aspirants appeared to the hand of the queen.

One was the Prince of Majorca, the handsome youth we have already spoken of: he bore her off triumphant over all rivals, including the son of the King of France. James of Aragon had one of those faces of melancholy sweetness which no woman can resist. Great troubles nobly borne had thrown as it were a funereal veil over his youthful days: more than thirteen years he had spent shut in an iron cage; when by the aid of a false key he had escaped from his dreadful prison, he wandered from one court to another seeking aid; it is even said that he was reduced to the lowest degree of poverty and forced to beg his bread. The young stranger's beauty and his adventures combined had impressed both Joan and Marie at the court of Avignon. Marie especially had conceived a violent passion for him, all the more so for the efforts she made to conceal it in her own bosom. Ever since James of Aragon came to Naples, the unhappy princess, married with a dagger at her throat, had desired to purchase her liberty at the expense of crime. Followed by four armed men, she entered the prison where Robert des Baux was still suffering for a fault more his father's than his own. Marie stood before the prisoner, her arms crossed, her cheeks livid, her lips trembling. It was a terrible interview. This time it was she who threatened, the man who entreated pardon. Marie was deaf to his prayers, and the head of the luckless man fell bleeding at her feet, and her men threw the body into the sea. But God never allows a murder to go unpunished: James preferred the queen to her sister, and the widow of Charles of Durazzo gained nothing by her crime but the contempt of the man she loved, and a bitter remorse which brought her while yet young to the tomb.

Joan was married in turn to James of Aragon, son of the King of Majorca, and to Otho of Brunswick, of the imperial family of Saxony. We will pass rapidly over these years, and come to the denouement of this history of crime and expiation. James, parted from his wife, continued his stormy career, after a long contest in Spain with Peter the Cruel, who had usurped his kingdom: about the end of the year 1375 he died near Navarre. Otho also could not escape the Divine vengeance which hung over the court of Naples, but to the end he valiantly shared the queen's fortunes. Joan, since she had no lawful heir, adopted her nephew, Charles de la Paix (so called after the peace of Trevisa). He was the son of Louis Duras, who after rebelling against Louis of Tarentum, had died miserably in the castle of Ovo. The child would have shared his father's fate had not Joan interceded to spare his life, loaded him with kindness, and married him to Margaret, the daughter of her sister Marie and her cousin Charles, who was put to death by the King of Hungary.

Serious differences arose between the queen and one of her former subjects, Bartolommeo Prigiani, who had become pope under the name of Urban VI. Annoyed by the queen's opposition, the pope one day angrily said he would shut her up in a convent. Joan, to avenge the insult, openly favoured Clement VII, the anti-pope, and offered him a home in her own castle, when, pursued by Pope Urban's army, he had taken refuge at Fondi. But the people rebelled against Clement, and killed the Archbishop of Naples, who had helped to elect him: they broke the cross that was carried in procession before the anti-pope, and hardly allowed him time to make his escape on shipboard to Provence. Urban declared that Joan was now dethroned, and released her subjects from their oath of fidelity to her, bestowing the crown of Sicily and Jerusalem upon Charles de la Paix, who marched on Naples with 8000 Hungarians. Joan, who could not believe in such base ingratitude, sent out his wife Margaret to meet her adopted son, though she might have kept her as a hostage, and his two children, Ladislaus and Joan, who became later the second queen of that name. But the victorious army soon arrived at the gates of Naples, and Charles blockaded the queen in her castle, forgetting in his ingratitude that she had saved his life and loved him like a mother.

Joan during the siege endured all the worst fatigues of war that any soldier has to bear. She saw her faithful friends fall around her wasted by hunger or decimated by sickness. When all food was exhausted, dead and decomposed bodies were thrown into the castle that they might pollute the air she breathed. Otho with his troops was kept at Aversa; Louis of Anjou, the brother of the King of France whom she had named as her successor when she disinherited her nephew, never appeared to help her, and the Provencal ships from Clement VII were not due to arrive until all hope must be over. Joan asked for a truce of five days, promising that, if Otho had not come to relieve her in that time, she would surrender the fortress.

On the fifth day Otho's army appeared on the side of Piedigrotta. The fight was sharp on both sides, and Joan from the top of a tower could follow with her eyes the cloud of dust raised by her husband's horse in the thickest of the battle. The victory was long uncertain: at length the prince made so bold an onset upon the royal standard, in his eagerness to meet his enemy hand to hand, that he plunged into the very middle of the army, and found himself pressed on every side. Covered with blood and sweat, his sword broken in his hand, he was forced to surrender. An hour later Charles was writing to his uncle, the King of Hungary, that Joan had fallen into his power, and he only awaited His Majesty's orders to decide her fate.

It was a fine May morning: the queen was under guard in the castle of Aversa: Otho had obtained his liberty on condition of his quitting Naples, and Louis of Anjou had at last got together an army of 50,000 men and was marching in hot haste to the conquest of the kingdom. None of this news had reached the ears of Joan, who for some days had lived in complete isolation. The spring lavished all her glory on these enchanted plains, which have earned the name of the blessed and happy country, campagna felite. The orange trees were covered with sweet white blossoms, the cherries laden with ruby fruit, the olives with young emerald leaves, the pomegranate feathery with red bells; the wild mulberry, the evergreen laurel, all the strong budding vegetation, needing no help from man to flourish in this spot privileged by Nature, made one great garden, here and there interrupted by little hidden runlets. It was a forgotten Eden in this corner of the world. Joan at her window was breathing in the perfumes of spring, and her eyes misty with tears rested on a bed of flowery verdure; a light breeze, keen and balmy, blew upon her burning brow and offered a grateful coolness to her damp and fevered cheeks. Distant melodious voices, refrains of well-known songs, were all that disturbed the silence of the poor little room, the solitary nest where a life was passing away in tears and repentance, a life the most brilliant and eventful of a century of splendour and unrest.

The queen was slowly reviewing in her mind all her life since she ceased to be a child—fifty years of disillusionment and suffering. She thought first of her happy, peaceful childhood, her grandfather's blind affection, the pure joys of her days of innocence, the exciting games with her little sister and tall cousins. Then she shuddered at the earliest thought of marriage, the constraint, the loss of liberty, the bitter regrets; she remembered with horror the deceitful words murmured in her ear, designed to sow the seeds of corruption and vice that were to poison her whole life. Then came the burning memories of her first love, the treachery and desertion of Robert of Cabane, the moments of madness passed like a dream in the arms of Bertrand of Artois—the whole drama up to its tragic denouement showed as in letters of fire on the dark background of her sombre thoughts. Then arose cries of anguish in her soul, even as on that terrible fatal night she heard the voice of Andre asking mercy from his murderers. A long deadly silence followed his awful struggle, and the queen saw before her eyes the carts of infamy and the torture of her accomplices. All the rest of this vision was persecution, flight, exile, remorse, punishments from God and curses from the world. Around her was a frightful solitude: husbands, lovers, kindred, friends, all were dead; all she had loved or hated in the world were now no more; her joy, pain, desire, and hope had vanished for ever. The poor queen, unable to free herself from these visions of woe, violently tore herself away from the awful reverie, and kneeling at a prie-dieu, prayed with fervour. She was still beautiful, in spite of her extreme pallor; the noble lines of her face kept their pure oval; the fire of repentance in her great black eyes lit them up with superhuman brilliance, and the hope of pardon played in a heavenly smile upon her lips.

Suddenly the door of the room where Joan was so earnestly praying opened with a dull sound: two Hungarian barons in armour entered and signed to the queen to follow them. Joan arose silently and obeyed; but a cry of pain went up from her heart when she recognised the place where both Andre and Charles of Durazzo had died a violent death. But she collected her forces, and asked calmly why she was brought hither. For all answer, one of the men showed her a cord of silk and gold....

"May the will of a just God be done!" cried Joan, and fell upon her knees. Some minutes later she had ceased to suffer.

This was the third corpse that was thrown over the balcony at Aversa.

www.ingramcontent.com/pod-product-compliance
Lightning Source LLC
Chambersburg PA
CBHW032229080426
42735CB00008B/770